RECKLESS ABANDON

A MODERN-DAY GOSPEL PIONEER'S EXPLOITS AMONG THE MOST DIFFICULT TO REACH PEOPLES

DAVID SITTON

AMBASSADOR INTERNATIONAL
GREENVILLE, SOUTH CAROLINA & BELFAST, NORTHERN IRELAND

www.ambassador-international.com

Endorsements

ALL I HAVE READ AND heard and watched inclines me to rejoice over the vision and theology and mission of David Sitton. I thank God for his Christ-exalting, God-centered, Bible-based courage to focus his life and ministry on the unreached tribal peoples. Like no one else I know, David Sitton puts his body where his mouth is. The risks are high; the reward is overwhelming. I commend *To Every Tribe Ministries* for your support and involvement. May the Lord of glory spread his fame through all who partner with this ministry to make a name for Jesus among the nations.

—DR. JOHN PIPER
Pastor for Preaching and Vision
Bethlehem Baptist Church, Minneapolis, MN

THIS BOOK WILL CHALLENGE YOU to reckless *abandonment* to the cause of Christ in pioneer contexts through a couple who have modeled it in their own lives. Read it at Satan's peril.

—DR. TOM STEFFEN
Professor of Intercultural Studies
Biola University

THIS IS A CLASSIC KNIFE–BETWEEN–THE–TEETH story describing how God called and moved out a man and his wife and family to take the gospel to the ends of the earth! You may not agree with every move or understand (or believe!) the stories, but they just might inspire you to step out IN your world or out OF your world to advance God's purposes among the nations.

—GREG H. PARSONS
Global Director US Center For World Mission
Pasadena, CA

THIS IS THE KIND OF book I want to read. It put me in touch with Reality. I was unnerved. I was convicted. And it fueled my soul-ache for God so that when I finished I couldn't help praying, "Oh, Jesus, this is how I want to know you. All I want my life to say is that you are real and you are worth it. Don't let me waste it!" There are so few of these kinds of books. Read it. You will not regret it, though you may get more than you bargained for.

—JON BLOOM
President, Desiring God Ministries

THIS BOOK IS AN EXCITING, true account of a husband and wife team, who from a young age, surrendered their lives to Jesus regardless of the cost. Whether one is young or old, the reader will be awed by this family's faith, courage and tenacity to preach Christ in indescribably difficult places where Christ is not known. As a mentor in David's early spiritual journey from hippie to man of God, I learned a critically important lesson, namely, one dare not dismiss the seemingly "little people" whom God can empower to accomplish great things for His Glory.

—DAVID E. DEPEW
President, New Life Advance International

I KNOW DAVID SITTON TO be a man who is willing to pay any price to walk in obedience to God. In the midst of much conversation about unreached people groups, I have known few people who are as passionately committed to the cause of Christ among the least reached as he is. It is that passion found in the pages of *Reckless Abandon* that results in a Christ-exalting challenge to the status quo of casual Christianity that will leave everyone who reads it changed!

—M. DAVID SILLS, D.MISS., PH.D.
Professor of Christian Missions & Cultural Anthropology
The Southern Baptist Theological Seminary
Author, *The Missionary Call & Reaching and Teaching*

Reckless Abandon

A modern-day Gospel pioneer's exploits among the most difficult to reach peoples.

Printed in the United States of America

ISBN: 9781935507444

Cover Design & Page Layout by David Siglin

AMBASSADOR INTERNATIONAL
Emerald House
427 Wade Hampton Blvd.
Greenville, SC 29609, USA
www.ambassador-international.com

AMBASSADOR BOOKS
The Mount
2 Woodstock Link
Belfast, BT6 8DD, Northern Ireland, UK
www.ambassador-international.com

The colophon is a trademark of Ambassador

Dedication
In Memory of Makayla Joy Sitton
December 6, 2002 – November 26, 2009

The story of the murder of my niece Makayla is told in a chapter in this book titled "Airmailed to Jesus." Makayla lived a joy-filled 2,490 days, loving and being loved. As my brother Jim, Makayla's father, said, "God knew she wasn't going to be here for a long life, so he compressed her days into a zip file."

Although she lived in Florida, not the jungles of Papua New Guinea, Makayla was killed, in part, because of her faith in Jesus Christ. It is extremely humbling to realize that my own niece became a blood-martyr for the gospel. She exemplified *Reckless Abandon* for Jesus and for things eternal.

It is my pleasure to dedicate this book to our sweet Makayla.

Continued Endorsements

"HERE IS A REMARKABLE STORY that I can relate to well--at age nineteen, a man exchanges his comfortable life for the danger and uncertainty of bringing the gospel of Christ to the often-hostile tribes of Papua New Guinea. In Reckless Abandon, join in David Sitton's amazing adventures and discover his passion for introducing Jesus to the world."

—BRUCE OLSON
Career Missionary (45+ years)
Author of *Bruchko*

I HAVE HIKED MANY MILES of jungle trail, traveled many miles of jungle river by dugout canoe, and spent many nights in tents and thatched huts with David Sitton. When he talks of the rigors of missionary life, he knows whereof he speaks. He's also a great storyteller. This book is a thrilling account of his life as a missionary and imparts his hard-won theology as well.

—ERNEST HERNDON
Author, *In the Hearts of Wild Men*

IN A SPEECH TO HIS military troops a president once said, "You are all dead men. Now go out and prove it!" This is David Sitton's "modus operandi." He is the real deal and this book is a testimony of his own reckless abandon, for the sake of God's Kingdom and the glory of God's Son among all nations. It is an exciting and wonderful story. But be warned, it is not safe. It may change your life!

—SCOTT WESLEY BROWN
Recording Artist, Worship Leader

OVER THE CENTURIES GOD HAS used missionary biographies to wake his people up. Some read and are called to carry the gospel to foreign lands in the footsteps of such bold pioneers, others are inspired to be missionaries where they live and work. This book is a compelling modern account of what God has done through one family. It continues the story of what Jesus has been doing through all generations. This might be the first missionary book you read, but I suspect it won't be the last. You will read about big sacrifices that are seen as no sacrifice at all because of the glorious worth of our Lord Jesus, and a hope that goes beyond the grave. Your emotions will be stirred. I found tears welling up in my eyes at times. You will read of violent opposition to the gospel being overcome by the power of God, and the relentless love of the missionaries. You will see again and again how God protects and empowers his people. There are specific examples of victories over demonic forces openly at work that remind me of the days of Elijah and the prophets of Baal. You will see that he who is in you really is greater than he who is in the world. Read this book and be challenged, encouraged, up-lifted, and provoked to serve Jesus in our generation.

—**ADRIAN WARNOCK**

Author, *Raised With Christ: How the Resurrection Changes Everything*

IN HIS NEW BOOK, *RECKLESS ABANDON,* David Sitton provides us much more than an exciting autobiographical journey through the life of an ordinary missionary. Instead, he allows his life's work to be the lens through which we see an extraordinary God getting glory for His name by magnifying his Son amongst unreached peoples. Written with candor and passion, David shows us the many joys and heartbreaks that accompany obedience to Jesus' command to disciple the nations. And make no mistake, suffering is part of the missionary call. But David encourages us--with story after story of God's absolute faithfulness--that Jesus is worth it. For all who are interested in God's great global mission, I highly recommend this book.

    —SCOTT ANDERSON
    Executive Director
    Desiring God

I FIRST HEARD OF DAVID SITTON when he spoke at John Piper's pastor's conference in 2006. I thought, 'Wow, this guy is intense,' which is saying something when you're at Piper's conference. I greatly respect David for his courage, his commitment to go where Christ has not been named, and his insistence on sound theology as the basis of strong missions. I look forward to reading his story of going, growing, and learning as a missionary. From what I've already read and from what I know about David, it will be quite a story.

    —KEVIN DEYOUNG
    Author, Pastor
    University Reformed Church
    East Lansing, Michigan

Table of Contents

Part 1
PAPUA NEW GUINEA

Part 2
STATESIDE

Acknowledgements

THE EVENTS OF THIS BOOK would have been impossible to live without God's endless mercies and miracles and the thousands of meticulous providences over these fifty-four years of my life.

I've got a great family! It is a blessing of God that my mom and dad are still with us. They both, in their own ways, continue to shape the man I have become in so many, sometimes humorous, ways. Most of all, they are lovers of Jesus, for which I am grateful.

My brother Jim and his wife Muriel have become my heroes. Over the last two years, they have endured a depth of suffering I cannot begin to imagine, through the brutal murder of their daughter Makayla, a story that is told in this book. I have witnessed my little brother stand before national and international news media, his heart pulverized to a daily bloody pulp of misery, from the death of his daughter, and yet proclaiming his hope and faith in Jesus Christ. In one of those interviews, he displayed violent[1] faith, by wearing one of our ministry T-shirts that proudly proclaims across the front of it: "Jesus is Worth It!" I don't think there is anyone that walks the planet that I admire more than my brother.

---

1   By violent, I mean that peaceful, non-physically violent, non-aggressive advance of the Kingdom of God. It's not an advance with shoe bombs and smart bombs, but the spiritual advance of the Kingdom that takes place when God's people "turn the other cheek" when struck, "bless" those that curse us and "forgive" those that harm us. It is the belief that we can, indeed, "love the hate out of people for the glory of God."

If you ever doubt that God answers direct, desperate prayers, look no further than my wife Tommi. There are not many that could have endured the kind of life that was imposed upon her because of the rigorous demands of pioneer church planting ministry. Doing double-duty raising children, enduring long separations and living all over Papua New Guinea in less than comfortable situations, and then coming home for a rest—which demanded constant car travel throughout the United States tramping through innumerable churches with three children in tow. Missionary wives are an awesome breed of woman! And Tommi is the best of them all!

Missionary kids often fall through the cracks of appreciation. Mine have endured the unseen sacrifices of long separations from their dad as he traveled the world on various ministry exploits. Grown adults now, Joshua, Barbara, and Jimmy are fun friends as well as my kiddos, and they continue to make me a happy and proud dad.

I also joyfully acknowledge those who have made this book possible.

Lynne Sonju Hertzberg assisted significantly in conducting interviews with me, transcribing my unruly notes, and organizing the material that essentially makes up the entirety of Part 1. Lynne also made the initial strategic contact with our publisher, Ambassador International. Lynne and her husband Hutz, one of my very best friends, have been encouragers and supporters of our ministry since the early 1980's.

My new friend, Vicki Huffman, my editor at Ambassador International, has been so helpful and encouraging to work with. In so many cases, she has helped me express more clearly on paper what already was so clear in my heart. I hope to work with Ambassador again on future projects.

I appreciate Scott Ronyak's computer graphic and photography skills. His assistance with developing the country maps and getting the photographs into useable condition for publication has been considerable. Scott, Kate and their kids are a valuable part of our "tribe."

Final, enthusiastic kudos go to my good friend and co-worker Margie Sanford. Margie is seemingly gifted in all things creative. She sees things. Perhaps, even more importantly for me, she shares my reckless vision for attempting absolutely impossible things for the glory of Christ and the advance of the gospel. It's a fact that this book would not have seen the light of day had it not been for Margie's encouragement, creative brainstorming and assistance with writing when I often complained that "writing a book is harder than living one!"

It's been said that "it takes a village," meaning, it takes a cooperative effort to do much of anything at a high quality level. For me, it takes a "tribe." I am incredibly happy and humbled by the team God has surrounded me with in this ministry. "Lord, would you continue to use our *tribe* and perhaps this book, to promote and advance the name of Christ and the gospel to the remaining unreached peoples of the world."

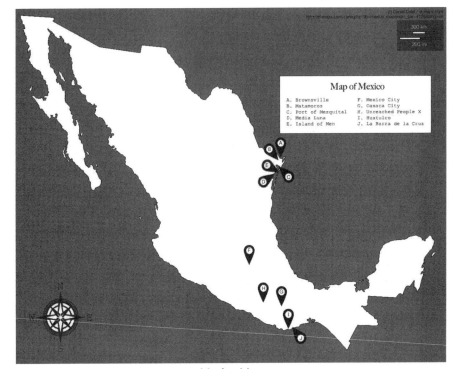

Map of Mexico

A. Brownsville
B. Matamoros
C. Port of Mezquital
D. Media Luna
E. Island of Men

F. Mexico City
G. Oaxaca City
H. Unreached People X
I. Huatulco
J. La Barra de la Cruz

Mexico Map
by Scott Ronyak

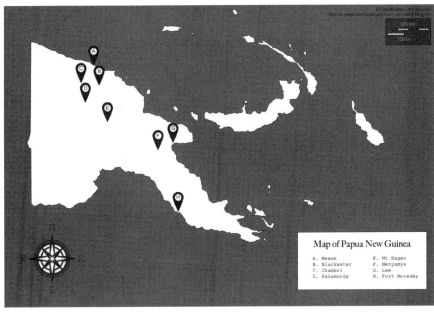

Map of Papua New Guinea

A. Wewak
B. Blackwater
C. Chambri
D. Rakamunda

E. Mt Hagen
F. Menyamya
G. Lae
H. Port Moresby

Papua New Guinea Map
by Scott Ronyak

Foreword

IN 1988, A NOVEL WAS published with a character in it based on David Sitton. About two-thirds of the way through the book, he is killed, beheaded by a New Guinea native.[2] He receives the martyrdom that has often awaited missionaries from the days of the early church till now.

Fortunately for us all, the real David Sitton is alive and well, and he would not only welcome such a death for Jesus' sake, but he actively recruits and trains pioneer missionaries who will have the same mindset and love not their lives unto death (Revelation 12:11). As he will explain in the pages following, this view of life and death (which he gets from his Lord and the apostle Paul) fills him with courage and frees him for ministry. He reminds us that risk is always determined by the value of the mission, and, from his point of view, Jesus is worth more than his life. This book goes a long way toward helping us all see that Scriptural priority.

Reckless Abandon is a riveting account of the wonderful works of God. His amazing providence and almighty power are evident on virtually every page. This will result in worship from Christian readers, so be prepared to pause and praise the Lord. But it should also result, at least, in wonder from non-Christian readers, inclined to explain things in terms of chance, coincidence, and luck. Conventional explanations are inadequate to account for what makes

---

2   Herndon, Ernest, *Morning Morning True* (Zondervan Books, 1988), p. 169.

a self-centered surfer kid into a fearless pioneer missionary, what makes cannibals into peace-loving Christians, what makes idolaters turn from the traditions of their past, and what makes men and women leave their comfort zones to reach dangerous places and people. In this book it is more than evident that "what" is the wrong word; it is "who."

It is Jesus Christ, the crucified, risen, ascended, reigning King and Savior, who, by the power of the Holy Spirit, changes peoples' hearts and reconciles them to the one that New Guinea people call "Papa God." The triune God—Father, Son, and Holy Spirit—is the hero of the book, and the gospel of Jesus Christ is shown to be just what the apostle Paul said it is: the power of God for salvation to everyone who believes (Romans 1:16). David Sitton has been a jar of clay with the treasure of that gospel inside (II Corinthians 4:7–10). You will read of that gospel at work, supported by acts of friendship and mercy, buttressed by power encounters, and under-lined by sacrifice and suffering.

As one who has been part of this story for the thirty years that our congregation has been David's sponsoring church, I can only say, "This is the Lord's doing; it is marvelous in our eyes" (Psalms 118:23). David and I have sat, talked, and prayed across tables in Texas, by the ocean in Papua New Guinea, and, as you will read, in a hotel room in Minneapolis. As I have advised him and sometimes argued with him, I have always been in awe of God using him. Over it all, triumphs and troubles alike, God was at work, molding a missionary who could and would train others to glorify God by taking the gospel to the nations. His legacy will live on, because it is really Jesus' legacy—the Great Commission itself.

Toward that end, it is a blessing that many of the amazing epi-sodes of David's life, which some of us originally gleaned from his newsletters and sermons, have now been set down in an orderly account. They have become almost legendary to those who have followed his career: the Kukakukas burning their weapons; Machete Bob's attack; the perseverance of Prisca; the baptisms of the ancient tribal chiefs in the sea. These are some of David's great stories, but they are most importantly God's great stories. They help us marvel at him, to have more faith in him, and to ask ourselves how we can glorify him.

This last question will be the one that this book challenges you to answer. Why? Because reading its pages is about to be part of your story, too. It could very well be that you may be inspired to put your life on the line for Jesus in order that those who have not heard of him may hear. It could simply be that you become much more aware of the need for greater prayer and support for missions. Perhaps you will realize that you are already a witness for Jesus and will endeavor to share the gospel more forthrightly. But I pray that the certain thing that will happen as a result of your reading is that you will be more convinced than ever that these words are true: "So, whether you eat or drink, or whatever you do, do all to the glory of God" (I Corinthians 10:31). Jesus is worth it!

—JACKSON BOYETT
Pastor, Dayspring Chapel
Austin, Texas

Preface

"Brother, there are whole tribes of people in New Guinea who have never heard the name of Jesus. Some are cannibals, some have pig tusks through their noses and wear grass skirts, many are wild, reckless and dangerous people. They don't know the gospel. Come with me into the jungles, swamps and high mountains. Let's go get some of them for Jesus!"

IF ANY WORDS COULD EVER be said to have changed someone's life, those piercing words from veteran missionary Joe Cannon changed mine. They propelled me at 19 years old to "drop my nets and follow" Jesus—to exchange comfortable South Texas living for the danger and uncertainty of engaging hostile tribes with the gospel of Christ in Papua New Guinea.

This is my story—the story of one who started out with little more than a Bible, a surfboard, and the assurance of a powerful God and gospel! As you read these pages, I hope you'll come with me into the jungles, swamps and high mountains—in many ways the "uttermost ends of the earth"—and discover what the transforming message of Jesus Christ can do.

Introduction

THE SUMMER SIEGE ON TIANANMEN Square in 1989 was temporarily halted by one man who dared to face-down a Chinese tank. It's an image that captured a century-defining moment of reckless defiance against the tyranny of communism.

One lone rebel, in another photo taken moments prior, was seen walking calmly through the frenzied, fleeing mob toward the enemy. He then stood unarmed, directly in the path of the advancing tanks. The lead tank tried to swerve around him, but he repeatedly side-stepped into its path with defiant, yet non-violent hand gestures. Rather than crush the young man, the tank eventually stopped its engine.

The peaceful protester climbed onto the hull of the lead tank, crawled under the tank gun to the driver's hatch and, on live

A "reckless" standoff with a tank at Tiananmen Square, China (Summer, 1989)
Used with permission

television, was seen talking to the driver. It is reported that he demanded that the tank commander, "*Leave my city. You have no right to kill my people!*"

The captain restarted the engine to carry on with his mission. But the man jumped off the tank and quickly re-established his bold stance, again blocking the forward progress of the tanks.

Moments later, three by-standers ran in to pull the man away, and they all disappeared into the crowd. It is believed that the gutsy young man was a 19-year-old student, who was abruptly arrested by secret police and became one of many that were brutally executed during the military crackdown in Beijing. He was never heard from again.

What are we to think of an incident such as this? Why would he be so reckless, knowing he would surely be executed for such foolhardy insubordination? Evidently, the atrocities of a communistic dictatorship were so oppressive that he was compelled to forfeit his life in an effort to stop it or at least to delay the inevitable, if only for those few moments he could control.

The "tank man" is to be admired. However, such risky heroism is not as rare as you might think. American soldiers overseas and firemen on the home-front often display similar "tank man" recklessness in their vocations. Lives are frequently sacrificed in order to establish a military beachhead or to rescue people from burning buildings. Somehow they muster the courage to endanger their own lives for others, convinced the cause is worth it. They risk their lives with *reckless abandon*. The dictionary defines the individual words this way:

> *reckless /ré-kləs/ adj: marked by lack of proper caution: careless of danger; utterly unconcerned about the consequences of some action.*

abandon /ə-bán-dən/ n: to give (oneself) over unrestrainedly.

When applied to the concept of mission, we can define reckless abandon this way:

> *reckless abandon /ré-kləs ə-bán-dən/: to give oneself unrestrainedly to the cause of Jesus and the promotion of His kingdom without concern for danger and the consequences of that action.*

By this definition, are we to be recklessly abandoned for Christ and the gospel among the nations? Or should we be more cautious? Should we only go into the world with the gospel where we can safely do so? What do we do when we find that it's impossible to manage the risks or to minimize the dangers to reasonable levels? Do we go—no matter what? Or do we wait until the red carpets are rolled out for us?

It is puzzling to me, as a leader in mission, when I am cautioned, even rebuked, by stateside believers that we should restrict our missionaries to only the "safe places." It seems as though many in the West believe we should attempt to engage only those people groups that present "reasonable risks" to our missionaries. The not-so-subtle assumption is that missionaries should be routinely evacuated out of danger zones.

Why is it presumed that *American* missionaries have the "right" to require safe living conditions? By the way, this is almost completely a Western concept. Believers in the rest of the world assume that following Christ is naturally hazardous to their health! They live as lambs among wolves, expecting to be mistreated because wolves eat lambs![3] Why do we think we should be exempt from what Jesus said would be the normal experience of His followers?

---

3   Matthew 10:16-25

If it is admirable for our military men to die on foreign soil for American freedom and laudable for firemen to risk their lives for citizens in peril, why are missionaries dubbed as *irresponsible fools* when they choose to remain in perilous situations with their families, "risking their necks[4]" for their friends and the gospel of Christ?

Here is my rationale for regularly sending missionaries with the gospel into hostile surroundings: Risk assumes the possibility of loss and is always determined by the value of the mission. The gospel is so valuable that no risk is unreasonable. Life is gained by laying it down for the gospel. If I live, I win and get to keep on preaching Christ. If I die, I win bigger by going directly to be with Christ[5] and I get to take a few tribes with me.

I conclude that "losing my life" for the gospel is literally impossible because my years on this earth are worth far less than the value of the eternal gospel. This is what Paul means when he declares: "I consider my life worth nothing to me, if only I may finish the race and complete the task the Lord Jesus has given me—the task of testifying to the gospel of God's grace."[6]

If this is true, there is no meaningful risk for me as a carrier of the gospel of Christ. If some tribal chief chops my head off, he's doing me a favor. Think about it. If I *get to* (not have to) lay down my life in some remote jungle swamp, but God uses my death as an object lesson to turn their eyes to Christ and His name and the gospel gets established among an unreached people group somewhere, that isn't a bad "risk" for me. I didn't lose; I won! It was the bargain of a lifetime because Jesus is worth a lot more than my little life.

---

4   Romans 16:4
5   Philippians 1:22-24
6   Acts 20:24

If we, as gospel ambassadors, are unwilling to suffer even as much as soldiers and firemen, could the reason be that we don't treasure Christ enough or value the gospel enough to sacrifice significantly for its advancement into unreached regions? Is Jesus simply not worth the risk to many of us? *Where is the line over which it is no longer worth it to go with the gospel?*

A Portrait of Reckless Abandon

Christianity is a graphic history of believers who lived with reckless abandon. They, the world might say, *recklessly* laid down their lives. Following the death of Christ on the cross, the deaths of His disciples have taken many forms: torn to pieces by wild animals in the arena, burned at the stake, hacked with machetes, killed with bullets or rocks or rope. But despite the bloodshed of believers—or possibly because of it—the gospel has won its greatest triumphs through the centuries. A cross-centered gospel requires cross-carrying messengers, and God has always had His messengers.

In 1956 searchers found the bodies of five missionaries on a jungle river bank. The "Ecuador Five" had been repeatedly speared, beaten with clubs, and brutally hacked to death with machetes by a gang of hostile Auca[7] Indians. Jim Elliot and Nate Saint are the better known of these missionaries. However, Ed McCully, Pete Fleming, and Roger Youderian were also significant members of the evangelistic team that tried to take the gospel to the Waodanis.

While they were students together at Wheaton College, Ed Mc-Cully had written an impassioned letter[8] to Jim Elliot describing how the Lord was compelling him to be a missionary. Ed was in law school and working as a hotel night clerk, but was unsettled in

---

7   "Auca" is the traditional name of the tribe, but it has derogatory overtones. The people are now, more favorably, known as the Waodani.

8   This letter, dated September 22, 1950, is included in its entirety in the end notes.

his heart about his decision to become an attorney. While he was walking and praying one morning, the Lord unmistakably sharpened the focus of his life to a single point. In the letter Ed wrote:

> Jim, I have [only] one desire now – to live a life of reckless abandon for the Lord, putting all of my energy into it. Maybe he'll send me some place where the name of Jesus Christ is unknown.

Five years later, Ed confirmed his heightened fervor for the desperately lost Waodanis in a simple statement scribbled in the margin of his journal: *I'm willing to give my life for a handful of Indians!*

And a few days later, Ed McCully and his four friends did.

Five good seeds fell into the ground and died on January 6, 1956—and the crops began to spring up. This single incident, widely reported in newspapers around the world, set into motion events that brought most of the hostile Waodani Tribe to faith in Christ. It also served as the impetus for thrusting tens of thousands of missionaries into virtually every country of the world in subsequent decades.

Statements by Ed McCully and the testimony of the blood-witness for Christ and the gospel of the Ecuador Five have frequently excited my own desire to live a recklessly abandoned life for the glory of God. I am honored to be one of the heirs to this missionary legacy and to now be passing the *reckless abandon* baton to a new generation of missionary "fools for Jesus."

Part 1
PAPUA NEW GUINEA

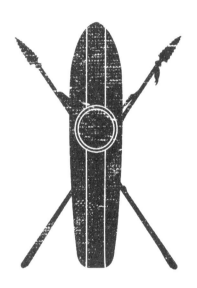

Chapter 1
Unlikely Missionary

IT WASN'T THE HALF-NAKED WOMAN breastfeeding her baby on one breast that captured my attention. Rather, it was the piglet munching down on the other breast that stunned me into silence. I don't know how long I stared at her. However, she stared right back at me, smiling and welcoming me to Papua New Guinea.

Hardly out of the airport, I had already encountered a situation that defied all categories, at least Western ones. It was the first of many shock waves that would soon usher in a whole new way of understanding the world for me.

Culture shock is the trauma of disorientation that occurs when one realizes that all of one's cultural patterns learned over the course of life are essentially meaningless in the new culture. It's a feeling of emotional imbalance and loss of equilibrium that confuses the newcomer. Thankfully, although unknown to me at the time, my transition through the stages of culture shock would not ruin my love for Papua New Guinea or her people.

Bob Herndon, the missionary assigned to greet me at the airport in the coastal town of Lae, had been running late and was worried that he might miss me. As he approached me at the airport, a modest landing strip surrounded by lush Papua New Guinea forests, he wiped his brow. It was hot, but it wasn't the heat that caused sweat to bead up on his wrinkled, tan face. Walking toward me—the only American in sight—he was undoubtedly concerned that he *had* found me. There I stood with my long blonde hair blowing in the breeze, a suitcase at my feet, a Bible in one hand and a surfboard under my arm.

Bob must have wondered: *Who is this guy? And what have I gotten myself into?*

And maybe I was thinking something similar. I'd come a long way from where I'd started, and I don't mean just the 8,000 mile trip from the U.S. to New Guinea.

Back to the Beginning

I was born in Fort Worth, Texas, in September 1957. My parents were cross-town high school sweethearts who were introduced by mutual friends. Following high school, my father enlisted in the Marine Corps and went to Okinawa for a year and a half. He was then stationed at Camp Pendleton in southern California. Only five weeks after I was born, my 17-year-old mother and I traveled to California by train to be with Dad. During my youngest years, we lived in Oceanside and San Clemente, California. Though I remember virtually nothing from those West Coast days, sunshine and salt water somehow got into my veins, and I've been a "beach boy" ever since.

When my dad completed his stint in the Marines, we returned to Texas where he got a job in radio broadcasting. Disc jockey jobs kept us hopping around small-town Texas in communities such as Mineral Wells, Kermit, and Lubbock with intermittent returns to the Fort Worth area, as he was promoted to larger radio stations. During those years, it wasn't uncommon for us to change schools a couple times during a year. My brother Jim (younger by two and a half years) and I apparently became rather pliable as we don't remember the frequent moves to be that grueling.

My mother, in my earliest memory, was able to stay at home with me but later worked for many years with Southwestern Bell Telephone Company.

In the summer of 1969, Dad was offered a sales manager job at a radio station in Corpus Christi. Some years later, he became general manager of KZFM radio and then transitioned across town into television in various sales positions. From 1970-1977 we seemed to move around constantly, living in at least seven different residences, but at least they were all moves within the city. We loved Corpus Christi and it became home for all of us.

Spiritually speaking, both my parents had been raised within the Churches of Christ, but we were sporadic churchgoers during the 1970's. My parents endured a stormy marriage for many years and finally divorced in 1973, when I was 14 years old. It was obviously a sad and difficult time in the life of our family. My mom, brother and I continued living together when my father remarried. On my 18th birthday, I moved into a small one-bedroom house, ostensibly to reside within the high school district of my choice, but I really just wanted to be on my own.

Murlyn Dowell: Spiritual Father

Most people who knew me during my formative years would never have imagined me becoming a missionary. My behavior negated everything that a good Christian life exemplified. It was the 1970's, and surfing, drugs and wild pursuits of the beach-going party culture were the passion of my life. Like most of my surf buddies, my existence revolved around the next wave, the next party and the next girl. I lived for my own pleasure and did it with gusto.

However, as a junior at Ray High School in Corpus Christi, Texas, I had begun to experience something unexplainable: a slow spiritual awakening. I still surfed, wandered from scene to scene, and spent a lot of time partying. Yet, I also felt a war within my heart. I didn't quite understand this *thing* that was gently wooing me away from the lifestyle I loved. On the outside I was cool, all smiles and quick to lose myself in the next beach bash. But internally I struggled with spiritual questions. Most of my life, I was literally basking in the sunlight, but I was restless within my spirit and as spiritually lost as a blind man desperately groping around in darkness.

Although I had a revolving door of girlfriends, I knew one who was different from the rest. Joyce Dowell was in love, but not with me. She was in love with Jesus. This surprised and even intrigued me. She didn't come right out and tell me she loved Jesus, but as I spent time with her and her family, it was obvious. Hearing about Jesus and the gospel, how he had come to earth to die in my place and save me from my sins, convinced me that the battle in my heart was the Holy Spirit calling me to Christ. What a thought! The God of heaven pursued me, and I came to realize that Jesus was enlisting me to follow Him just as He had called the first disciples to "drop their nets" on another beach far away.

Joyce and I always loved each other during our high school days, but never at the same time! We emerged from radically different worlds and,

David Sitton, long hair and a Derby hat (1975)

I think we would both agree that the Lord spared each of us "many sorrows" by keeping us more like brother and sister than boyfriend and girlfriend.

I joked with Joyce that I just "used her" to get to her dad! But I wasn't the only one. Murlyn Dowell's home was always full of people, mostly young guys. I teased Murlyn about his evangelistic abilities but always added that he had "great bait," meaning his four beautiful daughters that all loved Jesus passionately. His wife Icalee, "Mom Dowell" to dozens of us, was an additional attraction as she was the queen of hospitality virtually any time of the day or night and usually with home-cooked meals and incredible coconut cream pies!

Brother M.U., as I called him, was a spiritual grenade. I was going to say "fire ball" but that isn't explosive enough. As I eased into my new life of faith in Christ, brother M.U. leapt with both feet into the spiritual gap of my life. We spent endless nights in Bible study, prayer and non-stop dreaming of ways that we could live more radically for Jesus. We exhausted, no doubt, thousands of hours sitting on his couch, around his dining table or reclining on the floor underneath the piano studying the Scriptures. Thinking back, it was completely unnatural the amount of time that we spent together. It was "supernatural!" It was the nearest thing to "revival" that I have ever personally experienced.

Brother M.U. had a warped sense of humor that perfectly meshed with mine. We needed some humor in our lives as we endured unpleasant "persecution" from church elders that couldn't understand the spiritual vitality and radical Christian living that we were advocating. Oftentimes, when I was rebuked by the elders for something I had preached, M.U. would joke, "Don't worry about it, brother, you twist the Scriptures just the way I like 'em!"

M.U. owned a commercial equipment service company. He worked long hours and through weekends repairing elevators, dry cleaning machines and commercial stoves and ovens. It was hard, dirty work. One day, knowing I needed a job (not to be confused with *wanting* one), M.U. said he wanted to hire me to work with him. I said, "Brother, I don't know the difference between a screw and a screwdriver. I can't work in your business."

He replied, "Do you know the difference between the Old and New Testaments?" I looked at him as though he had lost his mind.

M.U. continued, "Your job is to carry my tools and talk to me about the Scriptures all day as I work on the machines!" That's what I did through most of one summer. I followed him through the day talking to him about things I was learning in the Bible. Then I had to study at night in order to have new material for the next day.

I don't think M.U. ever fully understood why I would feel compelled to go to Papua New Guinea. His desire was for me to stay in Corpus Christi and keep studying the Bible underneath the family piano. He even talked about purchasing an old Whataburger fast food joint and turning it into a 24 / 7 ministry house that I would lead. But the Lord had other plans for me, none of which could have happened without the spiritual stability and personal mentoring that brother M.U. invested into me.

When I left for PNG on the morning of October 3, 1977, M.U. and Mom Dowell were at the airport, along with my family and many friends to see me off. They were the last ones standing by the departure door. As I walked by them for last hugs, M.U. handed me a scribbled note that I still have today, and Mom Dowell pushed a coconut cream pie into my hands. I stumbled out of the door, eyes filled with tears.

Mom Dowell died of cancer in 1995, and I was privileged to preach her home-going. Brother M.U. died in 2004 from a brain tumor. Significant to me, he was buried on October 12th, the twenty-seventh anniversary of my first arrival in PNG. I was in Spanish Language School in Guadalajara, Mexico when he died. A few days before he died, he spoke his last words—what he would often say when we were about to be separated—"I love you, brother. Stay strong!"

M.U. prayed for me night and day while I was in New Guinea. The Lord used him, on at least one occasion, to save my life through his prayers. The Lord woke him up late one night in 1981 and put my name and face on his mind. He got out of bed, knelt and prayed, "Lord, there's trouble with Brother Dave over there in PNG. Help him, Lord!" Virtually that same hour, confirmed by our journal comparisons, I was miraculously rescued by a missionary helicopter when I was stranded among a hostile cannibalistic tribe in New Guinea.[9]

Brother M.U. would have loved the title of this book, *Reckless Abandon*. He was a reckless disciple for Jesus himself. Unorthodox, informal, tactless with the arrogant, merciful to the downtrodden; he was a radical Jesus follower that showed me how to be one too.

David Depew: Missionary Mentor

For the first time in my life, I was experiencing joy beyond anything I had known. True satisfaction came from knowing my sins were forgiven and Jesus' righteousness was mine. I no longer desired to live for selfish pursuits. I had an eternal purpose and destiny. As an unashamed Jesus follower, I pursued God with the same reckless abandon I had previously followed a hurricane swell on a surfboard.

As my high school years drew to a close, friends and classmates were making plans for their futures. I was eager to find God's purpose for my life, but had no idea how to discover it. Naturally, my father wanted me to attend college, but I had no desire for that. After all, I had barely graduated from high school!

I heard about a missionary training program, the *School of World Evangelism* in College Station, Texas, and decided that enrolling there might buy me more time to plot out my future. There were no visions for mission work, just a desire to

---

9   This story of rescue is told in the book, *In the Hearts of Wild Men*, Ernest Herndon (Grace and Truth Books, 1986). There were two significant results of this jungle expedition. Initial relationships, though strained, were developed from which a church was eventually established in Engati village. Secondly, I very nearly died at the hands of hostile warriors and from dysentery and black water fever (a usually fatal form of malaria).

go somewhere that I could study the Bible. I had no idea that a stint at this school would alter the course of my life forever, but getting there wasn't so easy.

There was a problem. I needed for my home church to provide references for me to accompany the application form. However, the elders of *Ayers Street Church of Christ* wouldn't recommend me. I sent the application anyway, with no references. When the director of the school contacted my elders for the reference, they adamantly warned him, "Don't take that David Sitton into your school. He's trouble!"

I was a new believer, freshly converted out of the drugs and surf culture in Corpus Christi, Texas and passionate about Jesus. The problem wasn't drugs and rebellion anymore, though my hair was still hanging down over my shoulders. The problem was too much passion for Christ, particularly my pursuing the fullness of the Holy Spirit in ways that didn't fit within Church of Christ understandings.

For reasons I still do not fully understand, the director of the school, David Depew, made a four-hour drive to Corpus Christi to meet personally with my elders. Once again, they warned him of the many sorrows that awaited him, if he allowed the rebel David Sitton into his school.

David Depew then met with me privately and asked, "What did you do to those men?"

Besides dating—or trying to date—their daughters, my only crime was trying to get Jesus into all of my life. It probably didn't help that my hair was still long and shaggy and I wore flannel shirts and blue jeans with holes in the knees. Not exactly the ideal missionary candidate. I was a young man who needed help. I had nothing to offer except a testimony and a love for Jesus.

David Depew needed to pray about my situation and returned to central Texas. In a few days, he invited me to visit the school. I cut off a few inches of hair and bought a new pair of blue jeans for the trip. I arrived in time to attend a luncheon for potential students and staff to meet and greet and have informal interviews. It was very uncomfortable for me. I felt like a "leprous hippie" among a bunch of "redneck Pharisees"! I overheard one of the instructors comment from another table, "Sitton won't be a part of *this* school!"

Against all odds, David Depew decided to take a chance and accepted me as a student in the school for the Spring 1977 semester. David told me, many years later, that the elders of the church that oversaw the School of World Evangelism weren't pleased about his decision to accept me. He was told straightforwardly, "If this goes bad, it's on you!"

Before my arrival for enrollment, I cut another foot off the length of my hair (though it was still not short enough for conservative Central Texas) and purchased a few pairs of corduroy pants. I wasn't going to disappoint David Depew.

As it turned out, I had very little trouble in school. The hippie was able to lie down with the rednecks in relative peace. I was a bit too theologically radical for almost everyone, but some of us became good friends and learned to appreciate God's grace and growth in one another.

David Depew was a West Point graduate and military paratrooper. Once converted, he and his family worked in church planting ministry for many years in Thailand. He has since mobilized many for gospel mission as President of *New Life Advance International*. He is a church planter; a missiologist; a mission strategist, a dear friend and now a frequent teacher and mentor to our students in the Center For Pioneer Church Planting. My children in mission are his grandchildren.

The Lord placed David Depew into my path to provide a pivot point in my life that set me on a course for cross-cultural mission that has taken me all over the world.

Joe Cannon: Church Planting Mentor

On a warm March day in 1977, I met Joe Cannon for the first time. Joe was a fascinating guy. He was tall and lanky with a full head of curly, gray hair combed straight back and down over his collar, and a complexion bright red with enthusiasm. Joe moseyed to the middle of the classroom with an armful of bows, arrows and spears while speaking excitedly in a strange language. He told thrilling tales of nearly inaccessible regions and uncharted mountain ranges. He enthralled all of us with exhilarating accounts of witch doctors, cannibals, and headhunters who had never heard about Christ in the remote jungle swamps. His message was mixed with both tearful passion and boisterous humor.

Joe was in his early fifties and had already been a missionary in the Orient for nearly twenty-five years, but he didn't want to talk about past exploits. He was captivated with his newest passion: the unreached tribes of Papua New Guinea (PNG).

I was entirely awestruck by Joe whose love for Christ and the gospel was palpable. It was obvious that he loved going to the hardest places and risking all he had to get the gospel "pioneered"[10] to the uttermost parts of the earth. I was riveted by the adventure of Christ-less peoples in far-away places.

After class ended, I stayed behind to talk with Joe who told me, "David, most people want to go where life and mission is easy, where they won't have to risk much. But I want to devote my life to something that will have eternal significance, even though it means hard

10   "Pioneering" the gospel was one of Joe's favorite ways of describing the missionary task. He also spoke of "spearheading" the gospel. A spearhead is the first part of the spear to puncture a target. This was Joe's concept of church planting.

Joe Cannon with Kukakuka villager   Joe Cannon with Kukakuka villager

living. God is sending me for all of my remaining days to find those who have never heard the gospel and to tell them about Christ. I want to go like the Apostle Paul, where Christ has never been named. I don't want to build on someone else's foundation.[11] That's not for me. I want to spearhead new ground for the gospel."

I immediately realized that Joe was verbalizing the increasing desire of my own heart. My pulse beat faster. Joe seized the moment with a straight-up challenge, "Brother, there are whole tribes of people in New Guinea that have never heard the name of Jesus. Some of them have pig tusks through their noses and wear grass skirts, many of them are wild, reckless and dangerous people."

He continued, "Come with me, brother. I can teach you. I can mentor you. There are not many who will go with me into the jungles, swamps and high mountains. Come with me. Let's go get some of them for Jesus!"

From that moment, the course of my life was firmly set. I would not go where the gospel was already planted. I didn't want to build

11   Romans 15:20-21

on already-laid foundations; I wanted to blaze trails in places where the gospel had not yet made its way. This was a mission I could really live for. I had enjoyed exploring remote beaches along the southern coast of Mexico that had never been surfed before. But now I would discover new regions where Jesus was not known.

When people ask me about the process of being called to the mission field, I am quick to say that I've been "called" to Christ, but I "go" with the gospel to the nations as Jesus commanded that His disciples do. I was never *called* to be a missionary. Joe sort of drafted me, but I joyfully volunteered. No special call was necessary. I chose to go…I wanted to go…I was compelled to go. It was a privilege to go. Where I go is determined by an open Bible[12] and a stretched out map of locations that still need to be pioneered for Jesus."

Papua New Guinea

When I met Joe Cannon, I didn't even know exactly where Papua New Guinea (PNG) was located. Yet here I was, barely a man, raring to go to this far away, dangerous land.

New Guinea perches like a pre-historic, bird-shaped island about 100 miles immediately north of Australia. Located in the southwestern Pacific Ocean, it is divided in half; PNG occupies the eastern half, while the Indonesian province of Papua (formerly Irian Jaya) occupies the western portion. New Guinea is roughly the size of California and is the second largest island in the world.

Papua New Guinea is a fiercely rugged land. Towering mountain ranges of more than 10,000 feet snake their way along the entire interior length of the island. Deep jungle ravines, canyons and gaping gorges explode with ferocious rivers that make foot travel impossible, except for the *bush bridges* that provide perilous crossings. A bush bridge is constructed out of woven vines and strips of tree

---

12   Romans 15:20-21; Acts 1:8

bark (today some are reinforced with rope, wire and sawn boards). They are built high over churning water and rocks and provide the only means of fording swift mountain rivers. Because of their elasticity, they sway with the wind and sometimes bounce crazily under the weight of walkers attempting to inch their way across.

New Guinea was discovered initially in 1526, but it was not until the late 1800's that Europeans built the first permanent settlements. Only in the last decades of the 19th century did gold prospectors and missionaries make regular contact with the coastal peoples and begin exploring the tougher interior. Throughout the island, there are approximately 1,000 tribes that speak more than 880 languages.

Less than twenty percent of the people live in urban centers, and the country remains one of the least explored on earth. Primitive, but sprinting toward urbanization, it is commonplace for many villagers to be wholly without electricity and running water. Yet, they actively use cell phones. The stone-age truly meets the space-age in Papua New Guinea.

October 12, 1977, just two weeks after my twentieth birthday, I arrived in this far away dangerous place with little more than my Bible and a surfboard. Only God knew all that was ahead for me.

: : : : : : : : :

Joe began my orientation at his kitchen table in

Departure for Papua New Guinea, October 3, 1977

Lae, Papua New Guinea, by sliding a burial form across the table to me. "What's this?" I asked uneasily.

With a husky laugh, Joe said, "Brother, I told you back in Texas. We'll be walking four or five days into the jungles and mountains. You may die in the bush or they may kill us when we get there. And if you die somewhere along the trail, I'm not going to haul your carcass back to the coast."

I shot back, "Well, I'm not going to carry you back either, you old man."

Joe was still laughing as he pulled out a second one, so we could sign them together.

Everything would be different in PNG. I should have realized this when I first saw that woman breastfeeding a pig but now, as I signed my own burial form, there was no doubt.

Joe and I agreed wholeheartedly that any discomfort, danger or peril we encountered for the gospel would be worth it. If one of us had to bury the other along the trail in some out of the way place ... it didn't matter. "Jesus is worth it. It would be a privilege."

David with three men from the Black Water
region – Looking for their villages on a map

Chapter 2
Kukakuka, Rakamunda

Explorers throughout history have taken extreme risks to trek through unmapped territories. Joe and I were part of a small group of the world's voyagers who endured hardship for the reward of unearthing treasure. However, you won't read about us in history books because we were not digging for gold or claiming land for earthly kings. Joe and I were hiking for human treasure, the souls of elect men, to reclaim them for the King of Kings.

"What about tribal villagers who have never heard about Jesus? Will God allow them to perish eternally?" This issue has been discussed and debated for centuries. However, there was no question in our minds. We believed that Christ purchased, with his blood, men for God from every tribe and language and people.[13] We were on a mission for the glory of God to find these redeemed people from among the inhabitants of the earth. The urgency of the mission was heightened by the understanding that many of those who had never heard of Christ were lost sheep that needed to be gathered.

Joe had information that the Kukakukas were a group who had never heard the gospel. This remote tribe was notorious throughout the Menyamya Mountains for their brutal practice of cannibalism. They were well-known for raiding exploits against enemy tribes, killing, raping, burning villages, and cooking warriors on rotisseries like pigs. One of the ideas behind cannibalism is the animistic belief that desired attributes of an enemy warrior—his courage, strength, deftness of foot and deadly accuracy with the bow and arrow—can all be acquired by eating the flesh of one's enemies.

I had learned that the Kukakukas first encountered a white person in the 1940's when a man tried to gather a population census for the government. He escaped with his life, along with two arrows for his trouble, one in each leg. About four decades later, Joe and I would be among the next group of white men to visit the area. We, along with several men from our missionary team, made regular visits to the Kukakuka villages. Over the course of many years much of the tribe were dramatically converted to Christ.

During one late night pow-wow with village leaders, the discussion drifted toward the gospel, specifically Jesus' metaphor about being "born again."[14] It was a startling series of God-moments as I answered their questions and moderated a feisty discussion while the men struggled to understand. I emphasized the meaning of godly sorrow that leads to repentance[15] of their sins and how even repentance itself is a work of God's grace within that brings about a change of mind and heart. Jesus compared it to being born all over again by the power of God's Spirit.

Once they understood, I began to press them about how following Christ might be verified in their own lives. If God was now truly living within them by his Holy Spirit, that meant they were God's children. If they were God's children, then they should be living under the influence and direction of God's Spirit and not the evil ways of ancestral and demonic spirits. I encouraged them with difficult questions:

"How will you know when you are actually living by the power of God's Spirit?"

---

14   John 3:3-8
15   2 Corinthians 7:9-11

"How will even your enemies see the reality of your conversion to Jesus Christ?"

"How will Kukakuka believers live changed lives that show love for enemies rather than hatred and harm?"

One of the chiefs picked up his tomahawk, pulled the stone out of it and placed it in the fire. He then reached for his bows and arrows and began breaking them apart, laying them in the fire one by one. As the other tribesmen watched the chief in amazement, they eventually began laying their implements of warfare into the fire too. It was a spontaneous expression of biblical repentance that would result in significant transformation for the entire tribe in the days ahead.

It was a memorable day when we taught the new believers about the significance of communion. Because of their previous beliefs about cannibalism, the truths of communion were especially meaningful to them. They wept as I read the words of Jesus, "Unless you eat the flesh of the Son of Man and drink his blood, you have no life in you. Whoever eats my flesh and drinks my blood has eternal life and I will raise him up at the last day."[16] Kukakuka believers wept over the greatness of their sin against God and for the unspeakable depths of spiritual intimacy with Christ through his shed blood on the cross, as expressed through communion.

On one of my later visits, I was told that two Kukakuka young men were

Kukakuka warrior

16   John 6:53-54

Kukakuka warrior

attacked and killed by a neighboring tribe. Their bodies had been carried back to the enemy village and cannibalized. The Kukakuka leaders gathered together and asked, "What is the appropriate Christian response to this attack?" In the past, they would have retaliated with similar violence. But, since they were now Christ-followers, they wanted to respond in a godly manner. Instead of running into battle, they chose to run toward a life free from the bondage of hate and revenge.

The Kukakukas are more commonly called Menyamyas[17] today, named after the mountain range where their ancestral land is located. The Menyamya churches are now into a fourth generation of believers; Menyamya children today are the great-grandchildren of the first tribal chiefs converted to Christ in the late 1970's.

The Rakamundas

After the encounters with the Kukakukas, Joe thought I was ready to venture out on my own with the gospel. However, at 21 years old, I wasn't so sure. I felt ill-equipped and inadequate to lead such an outreach. But Joe laughed and told me I just needed to go boldly and that the Holy Spirit would teach me how to be a missionary for Christ.

---

17 The *Kukakuka* moniker was what they were known as during their violent pre-Christian days and is often intended to be derogatory.

My first solo assignment was to lead a patrol to the unreached people of Rakamunda. To date, Rakamunda remains the most remote and inaccessible village that I have ever visited. Rakamunda is more than 300 miles from where I lived in the town of Lae. I arranged for a truck to drop me and my national team at Kubin Village in the highland boondocks of Enga Province. I would finish the remaining miles on foot with a guide, a translator and seven carriers. It was an exhausting and dangerous five-day walk through huge mountains and long stretches of completely uninhabited territory. My guide, a 13-year-old Rakamunda boy named Limb Jekop, had come to the town of Lae and heard the gospel. Once converted, he became concerned for the salvation of his people and convinced me to help him take the gospel to them.

Tingting Long Jisas Tasol

One young man in my entourage had the single task of hacking through the dense foliage with a bush knife to forge a passable path for everyone else to follow. The jungle was thick with weird-shaped trees, twisting vines and thorny, low hanging vegetation. It was beautiful from a distance, but physically and mentally challenging when in the middle of it. Jungles are never comfortable. One is constantly trying to avoid the prickly "gotcha" vines, and countless patches of poison ivy, while fighting off giant spiders, huge snakes, leeches, biting flies, mosquitoes and untold varieties of ants and centipedes. The deep-bush rain forests of New Guinea are an endless torture chamber.

I started out carrying only my water bottle and small camera. However, due to the rigorous climb, I quickly handed those over to my young friend, Limb. A walking stick is all I could manage. Two days into the hike, I was sick, fatigued and discouraged. My guide and carriers had all run way ahead of me and the trail was difficult to follow. I suggested to Limb that he should go on ahead with the others, but he refused to leave me. Limb was concerned that I might give up on the mission and turn back. He followed close behind me and at various, particularly steep points put his hand on my backside to help steady me and said, *"tingting long Jisas, brata, tingting long Jisas tasol."*

That meant "Keep on thinking about Jesus, brother, just think about Jesus."

We hiked up and down countless mountain peaks. Sometimes, we were on all fours for hours, climbing and scrambling over large rocks, slicing our way through the cold, wet forests. Then, we would slip and slide down steep inclines for hours on end. We would cross a stream or river and start the entire process over again, back up another mountain slope. Early into the grueling hike, I realized why the Rakamundas rarely ventured far from their remote village.

Finally, we stumbled into Rakamunda. The villagers were as stunned at my appearance as I was at theirs. Rakamunda men were bare-chested and wore bright green jungle leaves fastened around their waists with bush cords. The women were all topless and wore grass skirts. But, I guess I was the strange-looking one. Some of the people took one look at me and ran frantically into the jungle to hide.

"What is he?" whispered one woman as she hid behind some jungle foliage so as not to be spotted.

"I don't know," replied her friend, "I've never seen anything like him before. Is he one of our ancestors returning to us for some reason?"

"Maybe he's a god? Or maybe he's a man cursed by a god who is coming to destroy us," the first shot back.

"Be quiet, what if he sees us?" the friend nervously instructed.

They had never seen a white man and were convinced I was some sort of other-worldly, ancestral spirit. Limb called to them from the edge of the jungle, attempting to coax the people back into the village. He finally convinced some of those in hiding to come close to me. Slowly they emerged from the forest. Several of the women rubbed the hair on my arms, and licked my arms and cheeks to see if I was really human. The men's knees were visibly trembling at the sight of a white-skinned man.

After they were relatively sure that I was a human being, I gathered a few village leaders and began acquainting them with various things that I had brought from town. Every evening I would sit with them around a campfire in one of their huts. They were eager to hear all about my life and family in the United States. As days went by, I began telling them a few Old Testament stories, eventually culminating with the message of the gospel. I did this teaching in the Melanesian language[18] which Limb translated into the Rakamunda heart language. Within a few weeks, I had the joy of seeing several come to faith in Christ.

I made two more trips to visit Rakamunda over the next two years, and in time a small fellowship of believers was established in 1979.[19]

---

18 The Melanesian Pidgin language has developed as a necessary trade language in PNG in order to promote better communication between the tribes and with visitors from outside the country. The language is a conglomeration of several major languages, including English, German, French and Dutch, but is also heavily influenced by many of the 880 tribal languages which are spoken.

19 Unlike the Menyamyas, I have lost contact with Limb and the Rakamundas over the years and am unsure what has become of this remote and small group of believers. I still pray for them and dream of possibly connecting with them again someday.

David surfing in Puerto Escondido, Mexico (2007)

Chapter 3
Furlough Wanderings

AFTER TWO EVENTFUL, BUT VERY difficult years in Papua New Guinea, I returned home to Corpus Christi in 1979. I was physically very sick, having had numerous bouts with malaria, dengue fever and various types of pesky parasites. I had lost thirty pounds and most of my hair had fallen out—never more to return! Losing my hair so quickly was extremely traumatic as I had delighted in my long, blonde locks for as long as I could remember. However, it virtually disappeared down the drain over a short period of some months.

Despite my physical condition, I had become convinced of two things: First, I had to get back to New Guinea as soon as possible to continue pioneer church planting. And secondly, I needed a wife! PNG was a tough and lonely place to live as a single young man. I often prayed for a partner in ministry.

Dayspring Fellowship

I had been encouraged to get more education and had enrolled for a semester at the *Institute of Christian Studies* in Austin, Texas. A good friend from Corpus Christi, Carylene Dowell, the elder sister of Joyce (mentioned earlier), was a student at the University of Texas. Carylene rented a bedroom from a Christian couple, Ben and Lynnda Fletcher. She expressed concern about some of their beliefs, fearing they might be a cult of some sort. The Fletchers were part of a new church plant in Austin, Dayspring Fellowship, started by Jackson Boyett. And the "cultic" teachings turned out to be the completely orthodox *reformed* doctrines of *election* and *predestination*.

I began to attend the fellowship meetings of this small congregation which gathered in a barbeque restaurant. I didn't immediately embrace these "heresies" (at that time I completely rejected the doctrine of *election*), but I fell in love with the people. Jackson Boyett very graciously allowed me to share freely with the Dayspringers about my work in Papua New Guinea. My time with Dayspring was a sweet time of spiritual renewal. At the end of one evening, Ben Fletcher, asked me, "Brother, what are your needs?"

I bluntly replied, "I need a wife."

Ben chuckled and pointed me to what the group affectionately called their "prayer chair." They circled around me, anointed me with oil and prayed that God would quickly give me a wife who was perfectly suited for the tough ministry ahead.

Two weeks later, I was speaking at a youth meeting at a church in the south Texas town of Harlingen. Interestingly, at the close of the evening, the man in leadership asked the same question I had been asked in Austin. "Brother, what are your needs?"

Once again, I responded, "I need a wife."

The kids smirked and laughed. Three days later, back at home in Corpus Christi, I received a letter from a 17-year-old girl who had been at the youth meeting. The sentence that stood out was, "If you ever get back to this town, come see me. I've always wanted to be a missionary."

Over the years I've joked that I have never heard a more clear word from the Lord! However, the funny thing as I drove back to Harlingen was that I wasn't sure *who* I was going to see. Was she the blond, the redhead, or the pretty dark-haired one? She was interested in mission, and that was all I needed to know at the moment.

Fortunately for me, Tommi Anne Moses was the cute, dark-haired one. We became fast friends, emphasis on fast. I surprised her by showing up at a Christmas church service and that very night asked her if she would consider getting married and going with me to PNG as quickly as possible. Tommi made it no secret that she was willing to go. However, since she was only 17 and still in high school, her father would need to approve. Tom Moses was not opposed to the relationship but said unequivocally that she must graduate from high school first. That seemed reasonable. And I needed time to raise additional support for our continuing ministry in New Guinea. Support for two now.

Tommi graduated from high school in May 1980, and we married in June. I mentioned earlier that my hair had fallen out. Not living in a time when baldness was considered cool, I had felt constrained to get it fixed. There weren't a lot of options for a young missionary with little money. I ended up with a sick-looking pelt of a hairweave which I endured for a year. In fact, Tommi never saw me without it until after we were married. Great wedding pictures, I must say! Marrying me with that mop on my head was as *recklessly abandoned* as a person could be! I finally cut it off at a hotel in Hawaii on our way to Papua New Guinea. That hairpiece ended up as part of a chief's tribal headdress in the highlands of New Guinea. No kidding! But that is getting ahead of the story.

Jackson Boyett: Theological Mentor

When Tommi and I were about to depart for Papua New Guinea a few months after our wedding, we were still affiliated with the Churches of Christ. Before leaving, we visited Dayspring Fellowship so they could meet the young woman they had prayed for.

Jackson Boyett, the pastor, and Ben, an elder, asked us to meet with them. Ben, also the treasurer, informed us, "We have decided to support your ministry $120 dollars a month."

"No, brothers," I said. "I don't believe in election and predestination, and I *never will,* so it would be better if you didn't support us." Jackson laughed and said, "In that case, we will support you $120 dollars a month *and* we want to give you this stack of books!"[20]

I didn't realize it at the moment, but that's when Jackson became my theological mentor.

Tommi and I left for New Guinea a few weeks later. Back on the field, I began to read the books they had given me. Within fourteen months, I had studied myself into a theological dilemma. Finally, I contacted our home church in Harlingen, Texas, the same church where I had met Tommi, and my uncle, Robert Bostick, was the minister. I arranged to meet with the elders when we returned to discuss our theological differences that included my new convictions about the extent of the sovereignty of God as expressed in doctrines such as *predestination* and also my long-held views regarding the supernatural ministry of the Holy Spirit, including spiritual gifts and spiritual warfare issues.

I think my Bible was the only one in the room. They weren't there to examine the Scriptures; they were there to make it *official* that we were no longer supported by the church. Furthermore, they wrote letters to all of our financial contributors to inform the world that we were no longer missionaries. However, the church hadn't made me a missionary, and they couldn't make me cease to be one!

Tommi and I loaded up our orange van with every possession we owned, including our baby son, Joshua, and headed to Austin to find Jackson Boyett. We related the details of our sudden

---

20   These books included *The Sovereignty of God* (A.W. Pink); *The Institutes of the Christian Religion* (John Calvin), and the four book series (now in a single volume); *Foundations of the Christian Faith* (James M. Boice).

homelessness to Jackson and asked him what he was going to do with us. I said, "You got us into this with those books, now what do we do?"

From that day in 1981 until now, we have joyfully been under the spiritual oversight and care of Dayspring Fellowship. Through Jackson's sparse contacts with other reformed brethren, slowly over the next two years, we traveled in our ugly orange van through more than 35 states and to 125 small churches, rebuilding our financial support base.

We returned to PNG, ready to plant churches among unreached tribal people, in places where the gospel had never been established. Never could we have imagined that God would use us to plant more than two dozen churches over the next three-plus decades, including a small congregation among a remote and hostile tribe in the middle of a sago swamp.

Wedding Day, June 27, 1980

Chapter 4

A Woman's Perspective

MY WIFE TOMMI HAS HER own perspective on living and raising a family in Papua New Guinea, a culture totally different from anything she had ever known. Before I tell you more about our work there, I've asked her to tell you about the daily life aspect as only she can:

My part of our story began when I met David in the beginning of my senior year of high school (I had just turned 17) in Harlingen, Texas. He spoke at the Sunday night youth meeting at my church about his ministry in Papua New Guinea and life there. What I was most attracted to was his complete dedication to serving the Lord and his passion for preaching the gospel. He encouraged anyone in the group to write him if they desired. (I think he was motivated in part by the fact that there were a lot of pretty girls in our youth group!) So I wrote him (ink on paper–no email in those days) and we corresponded back and forth a few times.

On Christmas Eve, he showed up at my church and once again we hung out with the youth group. Unbelievably, David agreed to go Christmas caroling with us and out for a pizza afterward. I say unbelievably because as I got to know him, I realized how totally out of character that was for him. We hit it off and talked long into the night. As we cruised 77 Sunshine Strip in his blue Firebird and talked, he asked me point blank if I would be willing to get married and go to PNG for the rest of my life, because he wasn't interested in pursuing a relationship if that wasn't a possibility.

I was willing and told him so. But I added, "Let's not mention it to my dad just yet." As kind and understanding as my dad has always been, I figured this was pushing the boundaries just a bit and we should give this a little time.

David left the next morning, and we didn't see each other again until several months later when he officially proposed to me. After talking to our families, we began to plan a June wedding. My dad signed for me to get married since I was underage (David was 22), and I still had to finish high school. We married on June 27, 1980 at the beautiful Chapel by the Sea on South Padre Island, Texas.

David's dad sent us on a honeymoon to Acapulco, Mexico. Then we immediately hit the road to raise our support to return to PNG. I would not recommend this to a newly married couple. We did not often lay our heads on the same pillow two nights in a row for the first two months of marriage, traveling from place to place as David spoke in churches. We rarely stayed in a hotel, but rather in the homes of gracious people we were visiting. We had little to no privacy. What a welcome it was to finally have a place of our own when we landed in PNG in September 1980. We could unpack our bags, and I could finally cook a meal for my new husband in our own kitchen!

Home Away from Home

People, especially women, often ask about the physical living conditions. Our first home was in the town of Lae, Morobe Province, PNG. Lae is one of the largest cities in PNG. This is where David had lived before his furlough to the U.S. and was where other missionaries were also established. The home was a two-bedroom flat, an apartment raised on stilts with parking underneath. It was typical for the downstairs area to be fenced or gated due to "rascal" (criminal) activity. We had plumbing, electricity and running water. No air conditioning was necessary because the houses had so many windows and ceiling fans in every room. Rainwater was collected in 500-gallon tanks and pumped into the house. We had a bucket shower (with hot water heated by a kettle) in the bathroom. We learned to take quick showers and use less shampoo because when the tanks were empty, we had no water until it rained again. However, that rarely happened in Lae because it rained frequently.

I washed clothes in a twin-tub washing machine which I had to learn how to use. I put water and soap in the larger left side of the tub, and it agitated the clothes for several minutes. I transferred the clothes to the smaller spinner tub to remove the water and soap. Then I tossed them in a basket to await the next step. I washed several loads using the same soapy water because I had to conserve water.

Missionary Laundry Tip #1: Wash your cleanest clothes first! Tip #2: Don't toss clothes into the dirty laundry until you absolutely have to. Do the "sniff" test – if you can smell your clothes, it's probably time to give them a wash. Otherwise, wear them again!

After washing all the clothes and putting them through the first spin cycle, I refilled the left tub with clean water and rinsed them. Then I put them in the spinner tub for a final spin, hung them on the clothesline and prayed that they dried before the almost daily rain shower.

Because of the water situation, I never, ever, ran an open tap of water to rinse dishes. In fact, it was common practice not to even rinse dishes. To this day when I take a shower, I often shut the water off while sudsing up or shampooing my hair, even though we live in the U.S. and have an abundance of water. Some habits are hard to break.

Shopping for food was interesting. In the U.S. we can get most of our groceries (and more) at one store. However, in PNG it was not uncommon to go to one store for paper supplies, another for meat, another for cheese, etc. Then I went to the market for our fruits and vegetables. Convenience food was a thing of the past. Every meal was from scratch. Thankfully, a friend sent me a cookbook called More with Less written by a group of Mennonite women, full of recipes using basic ingredients. I have since passed that cookbook on to a dear friend now living in PNG.

Lady in Waiting

Two months after we arrived, I became pregnant with our first child. There wasn't a doctor in Lae, but once we moved to Mt. Hagen several months later, I found a Scottish doctor who did prenatal care and delivered babies. I was sick throughout my entire pregnancy, even to the day before our first child was born.

We relocated to Mt. Hagen in the interior of the highlands of PNG. We had a house built that was 14 feet wide by 24 feet long. It had one bedroom which took up most of the house, a 5x5 office, and a 5x5 storage room. The 5x5 bathroom consisted of a concrete base shower and a toilet (no sink – that's what the kitchen sink was for). The kitchen, dining and sleeping area took up the balance of the space. I hand-sewed curtains out of flat bed-sheets and covered the kitchen cupboards and windows. They were hung by nails and a string since there was no Wal-Mart to go to for a curtain rod. I thought they were lovely. I was very content in our first "owned" home.

Until we had running water, we had to use a bucket for night-time potty runs. That's when I earned the nickname "Bucko" from my dear husband (I was 8 months pregnant). He has always had a bizarre sense of humor. But, God bless him, he had a bed frame built and purchased a foam mattress for us when I was in the hospital after the delivery of our first child. Instead of coming home to a sleeping bag on the floor, I had a real bed! This was such a blessing because we had some pretty big rats that scurried about at night. When I would get up to nurse the baby at night, I would sit at the kitchen table and prop my feet on another chair so the rats would not nibble on my toes.

I thought everyone's first child came two weeks late; so I had been told. Two weeks before my 19th birthday and my due date, I started having contractions. Although I had read a book on Lamaze (natural) childbirth, I was completely unprepared. Thankfully, I wasn't even aware how unprepared I was. We called the doctor and he sent us to the "hospital." I use that term loosely. It was called a hospital because there were sick people there, but you didn't receive a whole lot of care from medical personnel.

The extent of prep for delivery was to scoot down on a bed, lift my maternity dress and push. However, my contractions had stopped before the baby descended the birth canal, and the doctor could no longer hear the baby's heartbeat with a stethoscope. He calmly told David, "We need to force delivery." What that meant was that the doctor had to use a type of vacuum to bring the baby the rest of the way down the birth canal, which in retrospect, felt like miles. Then he used forceps to pull the baby out.

When a grown man pulls a baby out of your body with all his strength, you might think it's impossible the baby is going to be all right. During this chaotic and painful procedure, I resigned myself to the fact that our child would not be born alive. However, what seemed like an eternity later, Joshua, our seven-pound, healthy, beautiful, little boy was born face-up with his umbilical cord wrapped 3 times around his neck. He had a swollen "cone" on top of his head from the vacuum and a cut on his ear from the forceps. He was crying—which meant he was alive! That was the most beautiful sound we had ever heard.

After delivery, the doctor left me and proceeded to deliver another woman's baby in the same room while I watched. I was never attended to again—no nurse checked on me following delivery. I had not been cleaned up, nor was I given a change of clothes. I was still wearing my blood-covered maternity dress. David had gone home with a migraine headache, so I was alone. After a difficult night with no pain medication, because the doctor told me I couldn't take anything since I was nursing, I was ready to take Joshua and go home. One of the other missionary wives came to the hospital to help me wash up and change my clothes. I was in a great deal of pain from the delivery and could hardly move. I stood in a freezing cold shower (there was no hot water) and she carefully and lovingly washed my body and helped me get into clean clothes. I learned years later that my doctor was not qualified to do C-sections. That would have been the likely procedure if I had been having my baby in the U.S. I was so grateful to the Lord for protecting Joshua and me through such a difficult delivery.

Thankfully, my second childbirth experience in PNG was absolutely nothing like the first. I didn't see a doctor until my eighth month of pregnancy when I traveled by plane to a larger city with better facilities to await delivery. David, Joshua and I passed the time playing tennis, scrabble, and cards. Barbara Anne waited until her actual due date to enter the world. I had a wonderful Australian woman doctor who stayed by my side, along with David, for the whole labor and delivery. I felt so good following this delivery that I could have gone back onto the tennis court the next day.

Our third child, Jimmy Don, was my only child born in the U.S. No complications and I had a hospital gown and a warm shower. Ah, such conveniences!

Living and Learning

It's not uncommon for missionaries to go through a period of adjustment when they first arrive at a field assignment. Most missionaries, including those who have had some preparation from a Bible school or sending agency, spend their first term on the field acquiring language and culture. Other than what David had shared with me, I had no training.

A few days after I first arrived in PNG, I started to learn Melanesian Pidgin. At a class taught by one of the missionaries, I was given some materials, which I was eager to study, so that I could begin to acclimate to my new surroundings. I had only had a few classes when David, who had been in the States on furlough for the previous year and was eager to get back on the field, took me out to Menyamya for a couple of weeks. This became a significant point in my language acquisition because I spent the entire time hearing nothing but Pidgin. I'd heard and can now testify that being immersed in language is the best way to learn it. After that bush trip, I picked it up quite easily and began to read the Pidgin New Testament. Within six months I was able to converse well enough that I taught Sunday School classes to children.

Because I was only seventeen when I arrived in PNG, I was young enough to consider much of what I was experiencing as an adventure. Although being so far from home and everything familiar had its stresses, it was also exciting. Missionary women introduced me to shopping in trade stores owned mostly by Filipino and Chinese merchants. These stores were equivalent to the old "five and dime" stores in the U.S. and were the places I shopped for household items or fabric. I learned how to get around on the bus system in the city of Lae for twenty-five or thirty cents. Both language acquisition and the ability to get around empowered me. I'm thankful that I jumped in with both feet.

One of the more difficult things for most missionaries to adjust to is the lack of privacy. As white-skinned foreigners, missionaries clearly stand out. People are curious. They stared at us constantly, watching everything we did, which was sometimes unnerving. In one case, it became more than unnerving. A man in Mt. Hagen began following me whenever I went into town. On multiple occasions he exposed himself to me! The situation was so distressing that I quit going into town without someone to accompany me.

Another stressor for many missionaries is the question, "How am I going to relate to people who are much poorer than I am?" Missionaries are the "haves" among the "have-nots." People are always asking for money or other things from missionaries. Most Papua New Guineans have a different attitude toward possessions than we do in the West. They freely share what they have and expect you to do likewise. If someone has a coat and you need it, they give it to you. This thinking is most likely due to the community-oriented way of living among tribal people. Unlike Americans who are individualistic and own personal possessions, New Guineans think that whatever belongs to one person belongs to the community. As an example, if I had a bicycle leaned up against our house, I would not be too surprised if it wasn't there the next time I wanted it. Someone taking a bike, if he needed it, was not viewed as stealing.

Once, when I had done a wash and hung three pairs of jeans on a line to dry, someone who didn't have jeans thought it was fine to take a pair off the line since David had three. Why would he need three pairs when I have none? This was a logical way for them to think, but it was a difficult adjustment for me.

It's not uncommon for missionaries to become insular when they are on the field, trying to protect themselves and their possessions. Some will stay inside their homes and close the door. These missionaries miss out on opportunities to develop relationships with people and advance the gospel.

Other missionaries have no boundaries and give everything they have: time, energy and resources. These gracious folks often burn out from lack of boundaries. No matter how much a missionary family may try to live similarly to indigenous families, Western missionaries, by virtue of their birth, are much different than those who have lived without basic "necessities." The challenge is to find and maintain a workable balance.

To me, it was stressful to find the right balance between compassion and creating dependency. We wanted people to respond to the gospel because of the message of Christ's salvation, not because we gave them stuff. David and I decided that we would live as simply as we could, invite people into our home for meals as often as we could, and respond to genuine need whenever we could. These guidelines helped us establish boundaries.

Dangers and Stresses

One of the greatest stresses on me was due to the nature of David's ministry. As a church planter among unreached tribes, he was constantly researching and visiting remote villages in the bush where I was unable to go, especially once we had children. There was no such thing as a cell or satellite phone in those days. When David left on an expedition he might say, "I'll be back in two weeks, give or take a few days." I knew that he was going into dangerous territory, facing illness, injury and hostile tribal people, but I had no way of knowing whether or not he was okay. I had to trust God that he would return.

Furthermore, in the 1980's, while we lived in Wewak, rascal (criminal) activity in the country was epidemic. It was not unusual to hear of missionaries and ex-patriots who were gang-raped. I was aware of a story about a husband who was tied up and forced to watch as a gang raped his wife and daughter.

Because we lived in a "fish bowl" and everyone knew our comings and goings, it was common knowledge when David left town. Since David had threats against him from people who didn't want him to spread the gospel, this added to the concern for our safety. Men would tell David, "We'll get your wife and kids when you leave town." When David left, I stayed with other missionaries or we hired a night watchman. Our home was broken into at times. Once, even though we had hired a watchman, he was held up at gun-point while the rascals broke in and stole most of our belongings.

To this day, I find it hard to relax with the sound of rain on the roof at night. When it rained in PNG, the rascals took advantage of the noise of rain on a tin-roof to mask the commotion of breaking into homes. David and I would often sit at windows on either end of the house on rainy nights to guard our home and children. On occasions, when someone would approach our house, we would yell out to them, taking them off their guard and frightening them away.

When people ask me how to pray for missionaries, I tell them that they need to be remembered daily, because these kinds of stresses are everyday realities. Pray for the big things: that the gospel will advance through their efforts; that they will be sustained through loneliness; that the Lord will provide financial partnerships; and that He will protect them from illness and those who would do them harm. But also remember to pray for the everyday things: transportation to the market, strength to do tasks such as washing clothes and making meals, finding correct boundaries in relation to possessions and privacy, and enduring the stress of long periods of separation. Pray for the Lord to sustain their relationship with Him and with one another. And, particularly, pray for their children.

I would not trade my experiences in PNG for any ease or comfort I could have had if we had stayed in the U.S. God used the years in PNG to sanctify me and make me who I am today. I don't think I would ever have realized how self-centered I was unless I had lived in PNG. I thank God that He stripped everything away to make me completely dependent upon him.

Chapter 5
Obedience-oriented Training

IN THE EARLY 1980'S, I became increasingly dissatisfied with the style of leadership training which characterized our ministry in Papua New Guinea. Up until this time, perpetually preparing and preaching messages and delivering them like a traveling circuit preacher among widely scattered churches occupied most of my energy. Though I had volumes of neatly typed sermons on file, this impersonal, Western approach of merely teaching classes and preaching to congregations wasn't producing the transformed lives and committed national leadership I desired to see. It was time for drastic re-evaluation and the formation of a different approach.

My job, as a pioneer church planting missionary, is not only to scatter gospel seed indiscriminately, but rather, to plant the gospel into new regions in ways that would produce deeply-rooted, culturally-relevant congregations of Jesus followers. Training men to be courageous and faithful leaders of their own people was one of the essential, but lacking, elements of our work in previous years. Flocks normally follow shepherds. My task, then, was to train indigenous leaders to capably shepherd their own flocks.

However, I had to do some quick learning myself. I was eager to blow apart many of the old paternalistic ways of working in which I had been taught, but I wasn't quite sure yet what to replace them with. The opportunity for a fresh start presented itself in 1984 when Tommi and I and our three-year-old son, Joshua, relocated to the beautiful small town of Wewak on the tropical north coast of PNG. I had explored Wewak a few years earlier as a young, single missionary when an Australian friend, John Moore, and I visited the town on a surfing holiday.

Now, no longer associated with the Churches of Christ, we arrived in Wewak with no friends, no contacts and no idea which way to walk out of the airport once we gathered our gear from baggage claim. Our first night was in the guest bedroom of an eccentric old German fellow named Rolf Stuttgen who latched onto us as we walked wide-eyed into the single-room arrival terminal. We later learned that it was his practice to meet every international flight looking for boarders in what he called a "guest house." Rolf was a kind man who gave us a tour of the town, and we slowly began to learn our way around.

Once settled into a small house, we purchased a four-wheel drive Toyota twin-cab truck, and determined to get busy with the gospel. For me, this meant serious praying that the Lord would teach me how to proceed. The experience I gained from Joe Cannon in the late 70's was invaluable, but I knew there was still a better way to work that was not so heavily dictated by the "white-skinned" missionary. I was painfully conscious of the fact that I didn't know the first thing about how to begin. But Jesus did.

A quick series of providential introductions brought three families into our lives that would become dear friends for many years to come: Leslie and Rose Minduwa, Edmon and Josefa Koski, and Rick and Lauren Velvin.

Leslie and Rose were from Yamanumbu Village, which is situated on the Sepik River six hard hour's drive from Wewak. They were new believers living in Wewak and interested in starting a church fellowship. Through Leslie and Rose, we became fast friends with

Edmon and Josie who were from the Sepik River village of Korobu. Josie began to work in our home with Tommi as a "house girl," which is a common practice in PNG. This afforded Tommi many great opportunities to disciple Josie. She became a trusted friend who often accompanied Tommi during those extended times when I was traveling around various bush locations researching places that had not yet been opened up for the gospel.

Rick and Lauren Velvin were from Auckland, New Zealand. Rick was the lead pilot for Missionary Aviation Fellowship (MAF) in Wewak, and he became a valuable resource for learning about new pockets of unreached peoples in the East Sepik Province. Our families enjoyed many meals together, and often Rick would pull out his detailed aviation maps and point out for me remote areas where the gospel had not yet gone. I chartered small MAF airplanes and Leslie often accompanied me as Rick dropped us off on lonely grass airstrips in mountain and jungle boondocks. Rick would retrieve us a couple of weeks later, after Leslie and I had tramped the hillsides in search of people with no gospel witness. It was an exciting time of primitive, pioneer gospel work in areas that were still virtually untouched in those days.

Four Statements = One Philosophy

A breakdown of Paul's words in Romans 15:17-24 is:

1. It has always been my ambition to preach the gospel where Christ was not known;
2. From Jerusalem all the way to Illyricum, I have fully proclaimed the gospel of Christ;
3. There is no more room for me to work in these regions;
4. Therefore I am going to Spain.

These four statements have greatly impacted my philosophy as a pioneer church planter. In about ten years, the Apostle Paul established churches in the four provinces of the Roman Empire, Galatia, Macedonia, Achaia and Asia. Before AD 47 there were no churches in those regions. However, by AD 57, about the time he wrote this letter to Roman believers, Paul spoke as though his work in that huge swath of four provincial territories was completed.

From Jerusalem in the south, all the way around to Illyricum (Turkey) in the far north, and west to the great city of Rome, in-

Josie Koski

digenous churches had been established in all of the strategic cities, complete with a plurality of elders in every church.[21] The task of completing the remaining work of evangelism was now to be left with those regional local congregations. The Apostle was eager to move on to other, still unreached, out-of-the way regions. Paul's attitude seemed to be, "There are churches in Rome, so I'm going on to Spain!" That was Paul. Never building upon another man's foundation, doggedly pressing forward, always advancing with the gospel into new places where Jesus was unknown.

The question of how the Apostle Paul established so many churches, so quickly, over such a wide expanse of land mass, churches that were able to carry on so well without his direct leadership is a fascinating one. The short answer is that Paul planted self-reliant congregations that did not revolve exclusively around him. The missiological word for this is *indigenization*. It's the idea

21   Acts 14:23; Titus 1:5

that new converts should quickly become culturally appropriate worshipping communities of self-reproducing disciples of Christ. This allows the missionary to remain a "pioneer" by moving along to other unsown fields. Otherwise, the missionary is reduced to becoming a "settler" that pastors a single congregation for long periods of time. Paul found ways to remain a pioneer and never settled down for very long.[22]

The antithesis of this missionary approach is *paternalism* which is the way much church planting has been done throughout the world until the middle of the 20th century. Unfortunately, this poor model of missionary dominance and national dependency hasn't been completely eliminated yet.

An example of a decidedly paternalistic ministry is from Ethiopia. The leader was an American missionary who essentially transplanted an American version of Christianity into Ethiopian culture. I listened to one of his messages where he referred to national leaders as his "preacher boys" and arranged every aspect of ministry so that it revolved almost completely around him. He did the preaching and teaching, presided over communion, monitored the finances and organized and led the outreach. Furthermore, even in the extreme Ethiopian heat that can sometimes reach 120 degrees, his "preacher boys" were dressed in long-sleeved white shirts and black ties. They had an American-style building, pulpit, and pews; they sang *Amazing Grace*, translated into a local language but still with the familiar Western rhythm.

This brother had simply cut a cultural sprig from an American version of church and cross-planted it onto the African continent. By his own design, he worked in almost total disregard of Ethiopian culture and worldview. It was the exact opposite of an indigenous or a *contextualized* expression of Christianity which would have incorporated appropriate architectural design, local

22   2 Corinthians 11:26

materials, indigenous dress and customs, and the use of musical instruments and styles of song and dance that were more culturally comfortable for a rural, tribal village setting. Not only was this expression of Christianity unwieldy, uncomfortable and largely without meaning on any significantly deep level for Ethiopian believers, it was not a reproducible or financially sustainable model once the missionary moved on, retired, or died. Too often, once the missionary is gone, local believers in churches such as this will either become harmfully syncretized, blending aspects of paganism with Christianity, or they will revert completely back to ancestral tradition and animism.[23]

My mentor Joe Cannon often quipped, "If you don't plant a church that you are somewhat uncomfortable with, you haven't planted a very good one." Joe's point was if the missionary is completely culturally comfortable with the church he established, it's probably a whole lot more American than it should be. Most missionaries, including myself, have not been taught how to work so that indigenous cultural forms and local artistic flavors can flourish.

Appropriate contextualization has nothing to do with altering the message of the gospel. We don't contextualize the gospel because it's already completely relevant to every culture. We contextualize the communication and cultural packaging of the gospel so that our converts, in PNG for example, would become New Guinean, New Testament disciples, worshipping within communities of believers that reflect all of the beauty and diversity of their God-given languages and cultures.

These are some of the difficult lessons I was beginning to understand in those early days of 1984.

---

23   A more thorough discussion of animism and the issues of syncretism and contextualization can be found in my book, *To Every Tribe With Jesus: Understanding and Reaching Tribal Peoples for Christ* (Grace and Truth Books, Sand Springs, OK, 2005), pages 31-44 and 81-99.

Hear and Do

I slowly but surely began to understand the genius of how Jesus interacted with His men. He was obedience-oriented[24] in their instruction. When Christ sent out the twelve and the seventy on their evangelistic patrols, He gave them an extensive list of do's and don'ts to follow. This is not a bad thing for new missionaries going cross-cultural for the very first time. Most new church planters I've ever known would have welcomed the advice!

Jesus commanded the twelve, "Take nothing for your journey, neither a staff nor a bag, nor bread, nor money; and do not even have two tunics apiece. And whatever house you enter, stay there, and take your leave from there. As for those who do not receive you, as you go out from that city, shake off the dust from your feet as a testimony against them."[25]

To the seventy, Jesus was even more specific: "Carry no purse, no bag, no shoes; and greet no one on the way. And whatever house you enter, first say, 'Peace be to this house.' And if a man of peace is there, your peace will rest upon him; but if not, it will return to you. And stay in that house, eating and drinking what they give you; for the laborer is worthy of his wages. Do not keep moving from house to house. And whatever city you enter, and they receive you, eat what is set before you; heal those in it who are sick, and say to them, 'The Kingdom of God has come near to you.' But whatever city you enter and they do not receive you, go out into its streets and say, 'Even the dust of your city which clings to our feet, we wipe off in protest against you; yet be sure of this, that the Kingdom of God has come near.'"[26]

No theoretical theology or methodology from Jesus. He didn't give them suggestions to consider. His men were apprentices who

24 I have borrowed the phrase "Obedience-oriented" from the writings of George Patterson.
25 Luke 9:3-5
26 Luke 10:4-11

learned through observation to obey His commands. They were taught to *obey without delay*. The result is they did not go out scratching their heads wondering what they were supposed to do next. Whether they were received as friends or rejected as enemies, they knew in advance where they should go, what they were to do, and even what they should say as different scenarios developed. They were expected to *do*, not just listen, to what He said. When the disciples returned, He gave them encouragement and corrective teaching, as they needed it, and sent them out again. This is how they learned to be missionaries.

The Apostle Paul took his training cues from Jesus[27] and I endeavored to learn this as well.

In the middle of 1984, a new convert named Mak Anis approached me with a request to help him take the gospel to his people in Rabiawa. About this same time, I was making evangelistic inroads into the village of Japaragua, which was only an hour drive from Rabiawa. I decided that I would concentrate the next couple of years in getting the gospel established in these two villages at the same time.

My plan was to spend three days a week in Rabiawa and Japaragua for the following two years. I ate and slept in their villages and gave these people the gospel, privately and publicly for about two months before there was any great response. Part of this was by design as I moved carefully through important Old Testament stories, preparing the ground for the coming stories about Christ and the gospel.

One night in Japaragua Village, I was reasoning the gospel in an open-air, thatched hut with 90 to 100 people crowding around two camp fires. We didn't need the fires for warmth as it was already excessively hot and humid, but we used the smoke from the fires as a shield from the monster mosquitoes. Later that evening, God did the "Lydia" miracle on twelve villagers, opening their hearts

27 Philippians 4:9

so they could repent and believe in Christ. Even deeper into the night, I huddled in a small hut with these twelve talking more about Christ and what it means to be a Jesus follower.

The next morning, I led these new

On-the-job training: Baptizing one

believers to the river with another hundred or so villagers eagerly following us with great interest. As I explained again the significance of baptism so the rest of the people could hear the gospel again and understand better about baptism, I splashed into the water and immersed the first two men. "Now you baptize your friends," I whispered to these dripping wet disciples. They began to backpedal out of the pond, wagging their heads violently left and right, saying, "Oh no brother, we couldn't do that."

I had them stand next to me and brought another dry convert into the water and demonstrated once more how to baptize a person.

Then, with fear and trembling, these two brothers immersed the fourth man as I literally placed their hands upon mine and together we took him under the water. These brothers readily baptized the

On-the-job training: Teaching two

On-the-job training: Never to baptize again in this village

remaining converts as I was drying off on the river bank.

The wonderful thing is that I have not baptized another person in Japaragua since 1985, nor do I intend to. I am quite thrilled, of course, to baptize my own children in the faith, but I refuse to make a habit of baptizing my grandchildren and great-grandchildren in the faith.

There is a great passage in one of Paul's letters that describes a practical aspect of his ministry.[28] I understand that Paul is dealing with a theological issue regarding division in the church in this text. However, we also get a glimpse into Paul's methodology. Paul didn't baptize all of his converts. Not even most of them. "I didn't baptize any of you except Crispus and Gaius." Then his memory kicks in, and he adds, "Oh yeah, I also baptized the household of Stephanas. I don't remember if I baptized anyone else."

Who was doing all this baptizing? It seems clear that new believers were baptizing the other new converts. Early church history tells us that 3,000 were converted and baptized on the Day of Pentecost, and thousands more were converted in the days and weeks after that. When Stephen was martyred, an incredible period of persecution came upon the entire church, disciples were scattered, the gospel was catapulted out in every direction and many thousands of new believers were swept into the Kingdom of God from Jerusalem, Judea and Samaria.[29] A large number of new believers were

28   1 Corinthians 1:14-17
29   Acts 2:41, 47; Acts 6:7; Acts 7:54-8:1

doing a lot of baptizing in those days, following the example of Jesus himself.[30]

From a strategic viewpoint, instructing our disciples to baptize one another may not seem so important. However, I believe it is noteworthy. If we don't train men in

David Sitton, leadership training in Rabiawa (1985

this way while we're with them, our disciples will find it all the more difficult to mature into their own ministries once we are gone. Typically, Japaragua would have just stored up baptisms, waiting while I was on furlough for me to baptize them when I returned to the field. That can make for an impressive newsletter, but we aren't interested in flashy newsletters. Our aim is to train men for ministry who can then reproduce themselves in the new places where they will carry the gospel.

One of the most exciting things to ever happen in our work was when this same fellowship of believers in Japaragua doubled in size from 60 to 140 people while we were home on furlough in 1986. They reproduced quickly because the ministry was theirs. I ensured before we left that they were already doing the preaching, they did the evangelizing, praying and baptizing. They served each other communion and oversaw the collection and its use, which included vegetables and fruit, as well as money. They were able to do all of this because I never allowed the work to orbit around me in the first place. Through behind-the-scenes, obedience-oriented, mentor-imitator disciple-making, Japaragua men learned to lead

---

30 John 4:2. The Apostle John makes special note that "In fact, it was not Jesus who baptized, but his disciples."

David Sitton, leadership training in Japaragua (1985)

the congregation. Because they were leading in my presence, it was not so difficult for them to continue to lead in my absence, and they have established new congregations in villages I've never even heard of!

I learned that I don't need to overtly be the "boss" of everything. Reins of leadership can be shared almost immediately, but always with a plurality of national men who are biblically accountable to one another and the church.[31] This is good biblical sense that will help avoid the all too frequent missionary experience of "baptizing 100 today, but not able to find 90 tomorrow."

A few years ago, on one of my annual return visits to PNG, I asked one of the Rabiawa leaders, Mak Anis, if they were continuing to quickly baptize new converts. He replied, "Oh no, brother, I don't baptize my grandchildren in the faith." Mak was already teaching his disciples to baptize themselves because he didn't want them becoming overly dependent upon him. I am confident that the churches in Japaragua and Rabiawa will continue well into the next generation because the gospel has been entrusted to faithful brothers who have gone strong for Jesus since 1984.

A Healing Word

Developing a biblical theology on how to manage sickness is another essential emphasis among tribal peoples. Tropical illness, especially tropical fevers such as malaria and dengue fever is rampant among peoples who live in lowland, mosquito infested areas.

31   Titus 1:5

Even in the highlands, though, many tribes have no access to basic medical care.

In addition to frequent physical sickness, many illnesses, accidents and unexplained deaths are attributed to evil, and/or ancestral spirits, or through curses and spells that are inflicted upon them by the village sorcerers. If a missionary fails to understand these daily tribal realities and does not clarify from God's Word the truth of His provision for bodily sickness, the people will naturally return to village witch doctors for relief.

Missionaries who are uncomfortable praying for physical healing inadvertently create an unintended assumption among tribal believers that God is only concerned about saving our souls when we die, but we are left to fend for ourselves in areas of physical illness and suffering. This false assumption often leads to harmful syncretism for tribal believers, such as energetically raising their hands and voices in praise to God when assembling with other Christians but then sneaking off to shamans through the week to get help with their more immediate problems. It is imperative that we develop a theology that addresses bodily illness and God's way of dealing with it, because if we don't, they already do!

Every tribal people group has numerous varieties of animistic "remedies" that are offered to them through witch doctors, sacrifices and exotic tribal rituals. Missionaries must understand the exploitative nature of animism. All of the sacrifices, spells, curses and rituals of animism are intended to maneuver evil spirits into doing something for the people, even if it is to only get temporary relief from their endless harassments. The over-arching truth to be stressed is that believers should pray in faith and submission to God who is our loving Father (instead of our trying to appease Him) as they are accustomed to doing in their relationship with angry, evil ancestral spirits through various ploys of manipulation.

One day I was privately discussing with three leaders-in-training in Rabiawa Village what they should do for the sick and oppressed people in their villages through a mentoring Bible study.[32] Subjects such as the symbolic nature of anointing oil and emphasizing that there is nothing "magical" in the oil, as they believe is the case with a witch doctor's potion. All of this instruction is intended to delineate the differences between the one, true, sovereign God and all of the lesser tribal deities they fear so desperately. Obedience-oriented teaching should include a private, practical demonstration, with the leaders, of different ways of doing ministry. Assume nothing.

One of the points I stressed is the fact that sometimes God heals in a miraculous way, but sometimes He doesn't. The important thing for us, though, is to always do what the Scripture tells us to do. If the Lord heals, praise His name. If He doesn't heal, praise Him still and keep praying. But always be faithful to do what Scripture tells us to do and leave the results with God.

After a while, I snapped shut my Bible and asked them, "Do you have any sick people in this village?" The men chuckled at the joke. Villagers suffering from sickness, disease, and demonic oppression are plentiful in every village. This was a perfect opportunity to put into practice what we had just book-learned together. "Okay, let's go to them." It's not enough to only learn the theory and theology. If we don't put it into practice while we're with them, how can we expect them to really know how to do anything once we're gone? Obedience-oriented teaching is all about creating guided experience through personal mentoring.

---

32   James 5:13-18; Mark 16:15-18. The larger context of this study includes the sovereignty of God and human suffering in general, as well as an emphasis upon God's power and superiority over all spirit beings and spiritual forces. More of this discussion can be found in my book, *To Every Tribe With Jesus* (Grace and Truth Books, Sand Springs, OK, 2005), pages 31-80 and 101-111.

Their initial attempts were awkward impersonations of me. But they quickly loosened up and eased into their own styles of ministry. When I left the village that day, I gave them an assignment to go into the huts of sick villagers every day for the next week until I returned. They were to anoint the sick with oil and pray for them in Jesus' name.

When I returned the following week, I asked them, "Did you pray for the sick?"

"Yes, but no one was healed."

I said, "Praise God, brothers, you were faithful to do what the Scripture said to do. Leave the results with God." The assignment was the same again for the next week.

I didn't go charging ahead, ready or not, into the next lesson. The end goal was not an abundance of information for the brain, not even biblical information. The goal was transformation of life. A lesson wasn't learned until it was implemented into consistent practice. A forgotten lesson was a useless one.

I gave them the same assignment for several weeks. One day, I arrived in the village on one of my weekly visits and the brothers were waiting for me at the road. They were shouting, "Praise God, brother, God has met us with power."

The Lord had graciously begun to heal many of the people in the village. But I was careful that my response was the same as before. "Praise God, brothers, I'm proud of you because you were faithful to do what God said to do. Leave the results with God. You aren't responsible when God doesn't heal and it's no credit to you when He does. Be faithful to God and the text and leave the results with God."

Today these brothers scrape oil out of coconuts, they pray for their own sick, they baptize their own converts, teach one another, serve communion to one another, and are busy carrying Christ and the gospel into the surrounding villages. Though by no means perfectly, Rabiawa believers are characterized by being "doers of the word, not hearers only."[33]

Tremendous progress in Christian maturity arises out of early participation in meaningful ministry. The key is to be repetitive and reproducible in your instruction. The less you are needed, the more successful you are. When your disciples can do everything you can do, and do it better within their cultural context, then you have effectively worked yourself out of a church planting location. This is the heart and soul of what *To Every Tribe* is all about.

Sitton kids, (l to r), Barbara, Jimmy and Joshua (1988)

---

33   James 1:22-25

Chapter 6
Leo Wasi and the Chambri

LEARNING HOW TO PLAY GUITAR had been a passing but recurring interest throughout Tommi's life. In the summer of 1988, she decided she wanted to pursue it more seriously. I began asking around our little town of Wewak, a community on the far north coast of PNG near the Indonesian border, for someone who could give Tommi guitar lessons. One night, I was introduced to a charismatic young man named Leo Wasi. *Wamburipinyuan*[34] was his tribal name. I first met Leo at the Windjammer Restaurant where he often entertained customers by singing and playing the guitar.

Leo was in his mid-twenties. He really didn't have a great singing voice but was tremendously gifted as a guitar player and songwriter. He could also perform in three languages. I was immediately drawn to Leo's powerfully magnetic and confident personality.

The way Leo lived and viewed life was not typical of Melanesians.[35] Tribal people are generally laid back and non-punctual,

---

34 Papua New Guineans have tribal names that are of deep cultural significance. However, most are better known by the "Western" or so-called "Christian" names that they have adopted. I make mention of some of the interesting tribal names of people in this book, but will primarily use their preferred Western names. For example: I was recently with some of my Menyamya friends that I haven't seen since the late 70's. I was asking about an old student of mine named Kwotolokwo. No one seemed to be sure who he was. Finally he raised his hand and confessed to be the guy. But he is now known as Steven and is slightly embarrassed by his tribal name.

35 Melanesia is a region in the South Pacific that includes the island nations of Papua New Guinea, Fiji and Vanuatu.

especially by western standards. They blow with the breeze and take life as it comes. But not Leo. He was driven, ambitious and punctual. Leo aggressively pursued his dreams to become musically successful and financially independent. He didn't want to be limited in life by the confines of tribal constraints.

Seeking an independent life and identity apart from the tribe was greatly discouraged. Leo was always trying to find the balance between being a faithful tribal member, while at the same time following his personal dreams. He complained often about the complacency of his people and their tendency, like crabs, to keep pulling each other back into the pot whenever someone tried to get ahead. Out of step with his own culture, Leo was a deeply conflicted young man. He could not have realized that he was about to become a dangerous lightning rod for trouble and spiritual controversy among his people.

As Leo and I sat talking between performances one night, I learned about the Chambri tribe for the first time. I had heard of the "Chambri Region" over the years but never knew there was an actual Chambri tribe. As Leo described them, it became clear that no witness for Christ had ever penetrated the region before.

I quickly scheduled ongoing guitar lessons for Tommi, so I could have more regular contact with Leo. As he taught Tommi guitar, I

Leo Wasi

began telling him about Jesus. Leo was a particularly inquisitive person who loved to learn new things. He was intelligent, spoke English very well and attacked his study of Christianity with vigor. He became a spiritual sponge, soaking up everything he could about Jesus. He critically examined the life of Christ, miracles, teachings, especially the parables, death, resurrection, and promised return. Leo read everything I gave him and peppered me with endless questions and friendly debate on every imaginable subject.

It didn't happen suddenly but, over some months, it became apparent that Leo had embraced Christ with genuine faith. With his fresh commitment to the Lord, which resulted in a radical re-examination of his life priorities, we became friends and constant companions.

Leo began to accompany me on weekly discipleship trips to the remote villages of Japaragua and Rabiawa in the East Sepik Province as I continued church planting in those places. These were precious times and strategic occasions to mentor Leo. But he wanted more. He wanted to preach the gospel himself.

The opportunity finally arrived for Leo to speak to a small group of believers in Wewak. But this was not enough for him. Leo wanted to preach Christ to his own people, the people of his bloodline, the Chambri.

The Chambri

The Chambri are a small tribe of about 1,700 people that live in three villages[36] on an isolated island in the middle of a sago swamp. Chambri Island covers approximately seventy-five square miles of mosquito, crocodile, and snake-infested swampland in the East Sepik Province. A fourth village of Chambri people is located in a settlement in Wewak. There were about 250 Chambris in Wewak at any moment, with a constant flow of villagers to and from their home villages on Chambri Island.

The Chambri live in thatch huts built five or six feet high on stilts to protect them from the sweeping floods and monsoons that sometimes crash through the villages. Chambri women do most of the fishing, while the men hunt and garden. Grass skirts, feath-

---

36 Kilimbit, Indingai and Wombun. These villages are spelled various ways, but I will stay with these spellings throughout.

ered head dresses, facial paint, and bones through the nose were a traditional part of the colorful dress code of the villagers, but they are now only worn during tribal celebrations. Shorts and t-shirts are common dress for the men and wraparound *laplap* dresses and t-shirts for the women.

Each of the three villages had at least three main clans. Several leading chiefs from each clan collectively govern the details of village life. These leaders were selected by one or more qualifying factors including: their ancestry, feats of valor in battle, or successful engagement in the supernatural world of magic, witchcraft and sorcery.

The Chambri were still practicing head hunters until a generation before Leo. He grew up hearing the harrowing stories of tribal fighting from his male relatives and admired the trophy "heads" that were sometimes displayed in the village spirit houses.[37]

On a drizzling evening in 1989, I encountered the Chambri for the first time. Leo and I drove out to the Chambri camp in Wewak hoping to speak to some of the people. Leo sent young boys as runners around the compound to gather everyone for the important announcement he wanted to make. I had helped Leo prepare a short message that consisted of his testimony and a brief presentation about Christ and the gospel. Leo constructed a bamboo pulpit especially for the occasion. It wasn't long before some of the villagers started to gather.

Tribal people love stories, and they listened attentively as Leo told the story of Christ paying the ransom for sin. As he transitioned from storytelling to exhorting them to repent and believe in Christ, a collective and palpable grumbling began to be heard among the crowd.

---

37   Spirit houses and haus tambarans are synonymous words. "Haus tambaran" is the Melanesian Pidgin word. These houses are also called "man houses."

True to his individualistic style, Leo resisted the expected tribal way of doing things. Sweat started to trickle down Leo's back as he felt the tension thicken. He ignored it and pressed on with his message. However, the groaning of the people became more boisterous. Leo continued to raise his volume, so he could be heard over the grumbling and cat-calls.

Suddenly, a man ran toward us swinging a tree stump and cursing Leo and me! "You must go, you must go. We do not want this message here." He yelled like a crazed lunatic as he kicked Leo's pulpit and sent his Bible and notes scattering.

"We will kill you and your families, if this continues," they shouted angrily as they punched, kicked and spat on us. The hostile group clamored around us, chanting in unison their loud threats.

I had taught Leo that if we were ever attacked when preaching, we should not fight back but simply do the best we could to protect ourselves from injury. As the punches and kicks flailed around us, Leo and I stood back to back with raised elbows to shield our faces and bodies.

Although it seemed like hours, the brawl didn't actually last very long before several older Chambri men stepped in to break it up. It was a disheartening end to the evening. Even so, Leo was already making plans for the next night.

I recorded in my journal:

> We had prayed for this opportunity. Leo spoke the gospel and I was so proud of him. He had obviously done a lot of preparation for this moment . . . He was devastated by the reaction of his people. I was surprised at how angry the Chambri men got about a simple telling of the gospel message. But, what a great start to evangelism.

I advised Leo repeatedly to be careful how he said things. "Don't needlessly incite them to anger," I would say. Nevertheless, Leo was eager to get at it again, and he had his own way of doing things. Leo was like a wild horse not easily controlled, which I loved about him.

The following night we returned to the Chambri settlement. Leo carried no pulpit or lamp. He held his Bible with a few notes in one hand and a small flashlight in the other as I stood beside him. However, before we could even get started, the man who had initiated the uprising the previous night, Joaquim[38] and several of his buddies came out to protest. Leo pleaded with them to just listen for a while to the message of God's grace and peace. They adamantly refused and a shouting match ensued between Leo and some of the more vocal men.

Seeing the futility of this approach, I grabbed Leo's arm and steered him away. The men followed, punching, kicking, cursing and yelling insults all the way. They promised to kill us if we continued bringing this unwanted message to their people. Leo's face was bleeding and his nose was broken as a down payment on the promise.

Afterwards, I scribbled another journal entry:

> We were fortunate to get out without major injury. They could have easily killed us, but by God's grace, we escaped. Planting a church in Chambri is going to be tough going.

As the weeks passed, Leo was continually harassed and beaten up, his family was ridiculed and his house was burned down. However, even with all this hardship, he persisted boldly in his witness for Christ to the Chambri. I was amazed how Leo, though often dis-couraged, did not allow setbacks to stop him. Instead, these rough

---

38 Joachim's tribal name is Maringkwai.

and tumble events drew him closer to God and more determined to get the gospel established in Chambri. I was inspired to observe my new brother writing beautiful love songs to Jesus, songs about faith and what it meant to suffer for Christ.

Leo knew his suffering was only temporary and that his pain was nothing compared to what his fellow tribesmen would endure forever if their souls were lost. He was compelled to persevere in getting the gospel message to them.

A Bad Beginning

In the past, when I entered a village, I would befriend and build relationships with leading men and chiefs before ever sharing the gospel. This is normally a wise church planting strategy. However, I had allowed Leo to convince me otherwise in our approach with the Chambri.

Leo thought he could reason with them about the truth of Christ. He was wrong. Since Leo had been so well respected among his people, I also thought they would listen to him. I was wrong. Unfortunately, our direct, aggressive approach brought about premature opposition to both the message and the messengers.

However, in the case of the Chambri, opposition to the gospel was inevitable. The Chambri, like most tribal peoples, were animistic. Animism is the fear of and worship of spirits, particularly ancestral spirits. It is the belief that spiritual entities and impersonal powers indwell inanimate objects and that all of creation is inhabited by these spirits and spiritual forces.

One important cultural difference between the Western and Tribal worldviews is that we in the West are truth-oriented, while much of the rest of the world is power-oriented in their understanding of the spiritual realm.

The Chambri's entire existence is concentrated upon brokering "temporary" peace with the spirit world. They constantly seek to please and appease the spirits through endless rituals, ceremonies and sacrifices.

Animism affects daily life in very practical ways. For example, the Chambri believe that a powerful ancestral spirit lives in the lake that surrounds Chambri Island. This is the spirit that provides the fish, turtles, snakes and crocodiles that are vital for their sustenance. They believe that worship, or at least appeasement, of this spirit is essential for their physical and spiritual survival. To dishonor the spirits would be disastrous. They are convinced if they don't keep the spirits satisfied they could be destroyed catastrophically.

Life has changed little in a thousand years for the Chambris. For millennia, they have lived under the strict tyranny of demonic spirits. Their entire lives are invested in endless attempts to placate demonic spirits through never-ending rituals. Sorcerers and shamans are commonplace in every village. Even the children have intimate dealings with these spirits on a regular basis.

Due to their geographic and spiritual isolation and the crushing grip animism exerts over them, the Chambri suffer under suffocating spiritual darkness. Chambri Island is spiritually infested with demonic spirits like termites eating through a rotted stump. The slightest glimmer of gospel light can sometimes motivate a whole tribe to revolt in terror against God's messengers.

As already mentioned, the Chambri were a headhunting tribe a generation ago. However, they didn't talk much about it with outsiders. In fact, they would squirm nervously whenever I persisted with questions about this part of their history. Despite their resistance, the reminders were all around, particularly at the edge of Kilimbit Village where four, six-foot tall stones stood erected.

This is the spot where Chambri warriors from the past would proudly display their victims of warfare. Following violent battles, tribesmen eagerly gathered around to watch the warriors chop the heads off of their enemies and drape the headless bodies over the stones as they danced around them with celebratory chanting to the spirits who had given them success in battle.

I had seen skulls on numerous occasions. Sometimes, I would see the trophy heads in the rafters of huts and at other times my Chambri friends would bring them out from secret hiding places in the cover of darkness for me to view. I was relieved that the headhunting days were over, since otherwise my head would likely be one of those on display!

One result of Leo's relentless gospel witness was the salvation of a Chambri man named Tio.[39] Tio's conversion caused a great stir among the people. A complaint was lodged that Leo's preaching was "disrupting the unity of the community." As a result, the Chambri leaders arranged for an open-air meeting with Leo and me at the Chambri settlement in Wewak.

Chambri villagers circled around us with obvious hostility. Some sat cross-legged on the ground, a few reclined on logs or stools, and others stood by trees chewing and spitting betel nut, their teeth blood-red from the juice. However, most of the people stood casually around us in a semi-circle watching the passionate interaction between Leo, me, and the tribal leaders.

"We don't want you preaching this Jesus to our people."

"But, we are here to bring Good News to you. We have a message of hope."

"We don't care what you have, we don't want you here. Do you understand? You are never again to talk to our people on Chambri Island. If you do, you will be killed. And that goes for you too, Leo.

---

39   Tio's tribal name is Pekjl Sikarapi.

You are one of us. We can't believe you've been deceived by this white man's lies!"

We tried to calm the crowd by carefully answering their questions. However, peace was not possible. The issues of ancestor worship, white and black magic rituals, and conjuring up spirits of the dead didn't leave much room for agreement.

Frankly, neither Leo nor I were known for tactful responses. I soon grew tired of the roundabout way the discussion was going and just blurted out loudly, "Jesus Christ is the only way of salvation – there is no other way. Believe in him or perish forever."

That set the crowd off into another angry fury. Leo and I escaped amidst shouted threats on our lives.

Through all the conflicts and turmoil of these difficult days, Leo continued to thrive spiritually. He passionately desired salvation for his people, and he was willing to endure heavy hardship in order to lead them to Christ.

Chambri Singsing, a tribal celebration

Chapter 7
Dealing with the Unexpected

"WHAT DO YOU MEAN WE can't return to PNG?" I said anxiously to the consulate officer. "I've lived here for thirteen years and Tommi for ten. Our children were born here. This is our home."

The government official, with a stern unsympathetic tone replied, "Your visas are being denied, and you can no longer live in Papua New Guinea."

His unexpected words coupled with the abrupt click of the telephone left me in stunned silence. It was 1990 and our work was beginning to make significant strides for the kingdom. The denial of our missionary visas was unforeseen and terribly disappointing, but we knew that we couldn't allow this to discourage the advance of the gospel. We would have to change course and continue on under these new rules of the game.

We decided that we would relocate to the United States, and I would make regular short-term visits back and forth to PNG. Without missionary visas we could not technically live there, but I could travel in and out with virtually unlimited freedom on tourist visas. Tommi might accompany me on some trips but would devote most of her time to raising our three children and assisting me with the ministry base in California, then in Texas.

This was definitely not ideal but seemed to be the best solution to a tough situation.

Incredibly, at the very same time we returned to the states, Dave and Connie Baker from Niceville, Florida were preparing to depart for PNG with their three teenage boys. They were planning to work with us! However, in God's unusual providence, we would not be there with them.

Dave Baker, an electrician by trade, had felt drawn to New Guinea for several years, but his wife, Connie, was adamantly opposed to the idea. David says that she told him that he was "clinically insane" for even suggesting such a thing! Yet, within two years, the entire family came to embrace the idea that God was compelling them to go to New Guinea. They courageously embarked on the journey to PNG and a tough ministry, knowing they would be on their own.

Dave and Connie arrived just in time to take up where I had left off. They were immediately immersed into language and culture learning and began teaching and mentoring the two new Chambri believers who were in desperate need of spiritual guidance. This was done with my limited assistance through phone calls and annual visits from across the sea. David eventually established an informal discipleship training school in Wewak to biblically train Christian pastors/leaders how to accurately handle God's Word when they taught and preached. Later, he and Connie began English literacy classes to further train national believers.

The ministry had changed, but the work would go on.

Taking a Chance

The Chambris had repeatedly warned me that if we ventured out from Wewak to any of the three villages on Chambri Island, we would be killed. All of my interaction with the Chambris so far had been at their village settlement in Wewak. However, despite the threats, we set our sights on Chambri Island.

One early June morning in 1992, Dave Baker, Tomas Kwaruk[40] and I went to pick up Leo and another new believer, Elias Sarin[41] in Wewak, to begin the trek to Chambri

David Baker (1994)

Island. However, there was trouble immediately. As we loaded gear into my truck, an old foe, Joaquim, came running out to oppose us. It was the same old routine of screaming, yelling threats and attempting to incite onlookers into a riot.

"You stop right now. We will kill you if you don't. We don't want your message. Leave at once." Joaquim continued to yell, but he was unable to rile the crowd beyond kicks, punches and verbal threats. Frustrated, he jumped into the back of my truck and started throwing our gear into the road.

Angrily, I jumped up into the truck and stood chest to chest with him. "Get off my truck," I said firmly.

"I'm not going anywhere. You are the one causing problems, and I want you to get out of here. We hate you, and we hate your message,"

---

40   Tomas Kwaruk was one of my converts from the early 1980's in Wewak. He became my most faithful co-worker in evangelism and church planting in the Sepik Plains area. He remains one of my most trusted national friends in the work of the gospel.

41   Elias' tribal name is Manginakwan.

Joaquim retorted. He was so angry that the veins were popping out of his stiff neck! His eyes were red and glazed, and a huge gob of betel nut[42] was hard packed in both cheeks. He continued his loud ranting and then paused long enough to spit a massive wad of nasty betel nut juice squarely onto my chest.

I was red-faced with anger but somehow able to maintain composure. However, Leo lost all restraint and got drawn into a furious and completely useless shouting match with Joaquim. Thankfully, the conflict never escalated beyond kicks and punches. Tempers eventually cooled and our team was able to get the truck loaded so we could begin our journey. However, we departed one man short. Elias, the newest believer accompanying us, counted the cost of the expedition and turned back. He realized that he might be killed and decided it wasn't worth it.

Dangerous River

The journey from Wewak to Chambri Island is long and grueling. It begins with a five-hour drive on a rugged, dirt road of never-ending potholes, some of which are large enough to flip a vehicle. Arrival at the village outpost of Pagwi is not the end of the journey. Pagwi is a pit stop, perched on the banks of the Sepik River. We left my truck in the care of some friends and prepared for an additional five hours in a dugout canoe down the Sepik River and across Chambri Lake.

The Sepik is the longest river in New Guinea, part of one of the great river systems of the world. It originates in the central highlands of the Victor Emanuel Range and meanders into Indonesia

---

42   Betel nut is grown throughout PNG and is used as a social beverage would be. When mixed with lime it becomes bright red and is so acidic that it eventually rots out the user's teeth. The smell is horrible (far worse than chewing tobacco), and it has an intoxicating element to it much like marijuana.

for a distance, before twisting and turning its way back into PNG, flowing north and eventually emptying into the Bismarck Sea.

The Sepik River is in the midst of remote, unspoiled wilderness. It has a subtle beauty about it, but there is nothing good about the swarming malarial mosquitoes. During the worst times, each team member is issued a dish towel that is rolled up and constantly used to slap their face, neck, legs and torso in a futile attempt to get relief from the tiny assailants. There is no law against slapping each other either, when the mosquitoes swarm unreachable parts of the body. Many of my shirts are blood stained from killing so many mosquitoes!

After days of brutal heat and constantly swatting biting flies and mosquitoes, it is human nature that tempers can shorten. The biggest challenge of these patrols, beyond the physical demand, is the spiritual and mental toughness that is required.

For this particular venture, I had arranged for a canoe to be ready and waiting in Pagwi. But, as so often happens in New Guinea, the boatman wasn't there. When he finally arrived, he didn't bring a large enough canoe. Then, to top it off, he had the audacity to try to renegotiate the previously agreed upon price. I don't have much patience for this kind of thing. It was my policy to never renegotiate a price in the middle of a trip. If that pesky precedent were set, missionaries would constantly be held hostage by unscrupulous nationals who would devise new ways to extort even more money from them. I don't re-negotiate during a patrol.[43]

"You must pay the price I say, or you will not have the canoe you want," the boatman insisted.

---

[43] I once poured kerosene and set fire to a 25 lb bag of rice rather than allow a carrier to extort money from me in the middle of a five-day walk. He threw the bag down and demanded more money, thinking I would either pay or leave the bag, which is what he really wanted. I left the bag, but not until I had set it on fire.

"But you already agreed on a price, and you know we had reserved the bigger canoe," I persisted.

"I have no recollection of that. This is the price. Pay it or leave it."

I ignored the boatman and proceeded to load the smaller canoe. However, it quickly became apparent that the boat was dangerously overloaded. In fact, as we continued to stack our gear, it started to capsize and some of the bags fell into the river. The canoe was far too small. It simply would not do.

The Chambri canoe captain sneered with satisfaction. It was already late, so finally, against my better judgment, I split the difference with the boatman so we could get an adequately sized boat.

After paying the "pirate," as I named him, we headed downstream on the Sepik River and then into a narrow canal which snaked through the exotic, low-hanging foliage. We often had to duck jungle vines and swerve to miss logs in the shallow water. Eventually, the canal spat us out into the sprawling Chambri Lake.

After all the delays, it was already getting dark and starting to rain. This was more than just a cooling mist; it was a tropical downpour. The water in the lake became choppy, and the canoe was tossed about in the violent waves, nearly capsizing on several occasions.

We were drenched from the rain but also from the waves that constantly crashed over the sides of the canoe. I had two concerns at this point: capsizing would risk drowning, encountering crocodiles, and losing important supplies. Secondly, being stranded overnight in the jungle could mean stumbling upon big snakes, death adders, wild boars or cassowaries.[44]

We were miserably cold and uncomfortable, but we persevered for several more hours and finally arrived on Chambri Island late in the night. Providentially, the noise of the rain on the thatch

---

44 Cassowaries are large ostrich-like birds that can grow to seven feet tall. They have black feathers, long legs and sharp, powerful claws that can completely disembowel a grown man with a single kick.

huts and the cover of darkness allowed us to sneak into Leo's hut without notice.

Leo's mother, Mata, fed us a meal of smoked fish and sago. Sago is a starchy root that grows in the swamps and is scraped out of the inside of the palm. Through an arduous process of extraction, grinding, repeated washing and massaging, it becomes a sticky paste. It is then either baked into a bread or pancake consistency or steamed into a dark gray jelly-textured pudding. Truly, there is no American equivalent. The taste is often described by westerners as unpalatable. Over the years, I learned to eat most New Guinean food (including grub worms), but sago had always been a struggle to eat. However, after this long day and night on the river, even sago was welcome.

Mata's hut was like most in the village, elevated about five feet off the ground. The floor was made from strips of sago palm called *limbum*. The walls were draped with mosquito nets, which were collapsed during the day to allow more space for moving around. The one large room that made up the hut was bare except for a large clay cooking pot in the far corner and a few carved stools (about knee high) where the adults could sit. At night, everyone slept on bamboo mats, with a light sheet and a mosquito net around them.

The hut provided a wonderful reprieve from the violent storm, and we enjoyed warming ourselves by the fire as we discussed a strategy. Since the following day was Saturday, the big market day of the week, Leo suggested we walk through all three villages and greet the people. Then, at the end of the day, when the market was at its busiest, we could find a prominent place to preach the gospel for all to hear. Although I had some reservations about this plan, I was willing to follow Leo's lead since these were his people and his home village. However, I knew very well that we would, once again, be going against recommended procedure.

The next morning, we awakened to a beautiful clear blue sky and lots of sunshine. It was a pleasant jungle morning, except for the militant buzzing of mosquitoes. We squirted mosquito spray and rubbed lotions on our bodies and then started walking through Kilimbit Village, stopping to talk with people along the way. Most of the villagers were pleasant and many smiled and waved. Some yelled early morning greetings to us.

Leo provided quick biographies of the various people we encountered on the trail and showed us special points of interest along the way. He paused at a small stone marker that was the dividing line between the Kilimbit and Indingai villages. The stone marked the burial place of an important Chambri ancestor named *Toon*.

As we walked through Indingai Village, people became more agitated, hurling insults and veiled threats as well as a few rocks. Even the children standing along the edge of the jungle launched rocks at us with their catapult slingshots.

Sadly, near the border of the Indingai and Wombun villages, Leo suddenly lost his courage and refused to walk any further. It was a disappointment to see this normally strong and brave man succumb to his fears. Only Dave Baker and Tomas would go forward with me.

When we arrived at Wombun village, I began talking to a small group of men near the market, but was soon shouted down and jeered. One man in particular, Linus, was adamantly opposed to me and my friends being there. Some of these people were from the group of Chambris in Wewak who followed us to Chambri Island armed with machetes, ready to disrupt any gatherings that we initiated. They surrounded us, yelled curses and tried to intimidate us.

For whatever reason, they didn't harm us, even though they made plenty of noise about being there to "kill the missionaries."

By the end of the day the Lord had opened the heart of Linus and prompted him to come visit us that night. I was able to talk with him at length about the magnificence of the saving work of Christ on the cross and what it would mean to be a disciple of Christ. The Lord seemed to be softening his heart towards us.

From this time on, the Chambri leaders were quietly defiant toward me. The village men had nearly followed through on their vows of violence. But now, they gathered frequently in the spirit house discussing how they could manage the intrusion of this new "religion" we had brought.

One night, Leo was summoned before the village council to discuss the matter further. They rebuked him for trying to bring Christianity into the Chambri villages. He remained silent for a long time. Then, he respectfully and calmly responded, "I am going to bring Jesus to my people." After that, he turned around and quietly walked out of the meeting.

Early the next morning, Leo was once again summoned before the elders. They told him they had argued through the night about his situation. However, much to his surprise, they said since he had been respectful and had not fought back the day before, they would not hinder him from bringing news of Jesus among the Chambri.

Leo, David Baker, and I had been careful to respond to the Chambri attacks and abuse with love and kindness. Our motto was quite simply to "love the hate out of them." We were encouraged to think it might be working.

Chapter 8

Movie Magic and Gospel Seed

IT HAD BEEN A YEAR since the riot at the Chambri compound in Wewak when I decided to venture out there again, this time to show the *Jesus* film that had recently been produced in the Melanesian language. Ironically, the projector was set up less than fifty feet from where the previous year's uprising had taken place.

Only a few people showed up at first. But as it got dark, more than 200 Chambris could be seen scattered around. Even some who had been part of the riots a year earlier were spotted hiding behind my truck, watching intently.

The difficult part of getting them to watch the movie initially, believe it or not, was to convince them that the technology wasn't some sort of white man's "magic." Many of the people had never seen a movie projector at that time, and it frightened them to see "little people" moving around on a sheet that we had stretched out to use as a screen. However, once they were persuaded it was safe, they eagerly watched the story of Jesus.

As the film concluded with the ascension of Christ, I gave a brief explanation of the gospel and exhorted the people to repent and believe in Christ. Gospel tracts had been prepared in Melanesian, and the people grabbed them out of our hands with gusto.

Dave had consistently mentored Elias, and he was flourishing spiritually. In fact, Leo and Elias were now leading the charge for Christ among the Chambri. Dave and Connie built a hut for themselves on Chambri Island so they could stay for extended periods. The Chambri came to view the Bakers as dear friends. They could often be seen working, laughing, cooking and eating together. David became so well respected that he was invited into the Kilimbit spirit house. This was truly an honor as these spirit houses were traditionally intended for the exclusive use of the initiated men.

Spirit houses were the center point in each village and the most visually recognizable and strategically situated structure in the community. The houses were supported by tall pillars and long, heavy horizontal cross-beams that were intricately carved and hand-painted. Some of the carvings were so ancient that even the oldest chief didn't know who carved them or the legend that they represented. Many of the details were forgotten, but the images themselves were still revered—and even feared.

The houses were about sixty by forty feet with long elevated benches running along the periphery of both sides of the hut. The men sat on these platforms in groups, according to their clan affinities. Well-stoked campfires burned in two or three places, partly using the smoke as a shield against mosquitoes, but also allowing them to boil coffee, roast bananas or reheat smoked fish. Several large, slit-gong garamut drums sat prominently in the middle of the men. They sometimes beat on these drums with long poles, beating out tribal rhythms or even sending messages to men in other villages. In the old days,

Village Spirit House

garamut drums were sometimes used, when they were confident of victory, to announce attacks on enemy villages.

Traditionally, women were not allowed to enter spirit houses at any time, and they knew all too well they could be killed if they even got too close. They were even forbidden to walk on the paths nearby.

Important village decisions were made in spirit houses. Social and religious debates also took place there, but only the initiated men were ever allowed to participate in those discussions.

One late afternoon, Dave Baker was summoned to the spirit house for the first time. He had no idea the opportunity which was about to be given to him. As he sat with the men, one of the leaders asked him, "Dave, do you have any stories?"

"Yes," he replied, "what type of stories do you want to hear?"

"Any."

Dave began telling them the story of Abraham, an old man who had no children. He knew that to the Chambri, being childless was the greatest curse one could suffer. They were captivated as Dave told them how this man's God had visited him and assured him, that even though he was very old, he would have a son who would also have many sons and daughters.

Exclamation is expressed among the Chambri by making a clicking sound with the tongue, and Dave could hear clicking throughout the spirit house.

He went on to tell how happy the mother and father had been when the baby was born and grew to be a strong and smart son. But then one day the man's God visited him again and made a request. "I want you to take this boy, the one I promised would be the father of many children, and go to a mountain and cut his throat and burn his body to ash."[45]

---

45 Gen. 22:2

Every Chambri man was speechless. This was an unimaginable request even in their culture, and they were absolutely stunned that the father was willing to do it. But, what relief they felt when they heard that the man's God stopped him from going through with the slaughter and instead provided an animal for the sacrifice.

The Chambri men listened earnestly as Dave spoke and asked many questions when he finished the story. The next morning, Dave went back into the *haus tambaran*, this time uninvited, and sat down. Within minutes he was asked if he had any more stories. Over the next four and half hours, he shared as many Bible stories as he could think of. The men sat captivated and concentrated on every word.

It seemed as though there was a spiritual stirring among the key men of the village. It was hard to believe that some of the very same men who had tried to kill us in days past were now interested in these gospel discussions.

Transformation Begins

In early 1994, Elias began to feel a burden to return to Chambri Island full time in an effort to see the church fully established there. He thought his presence would make a strong statement, especially since Leo Wasi had relocated to another area of the country to pursue his musical career. Elias moved his family back to Kilimbit Village and built a new thatch hut for them.

Dave met regularly with Elias to continue mentoring him, while at the same time Elias began discipling and teaching the four other Chambri believers. Dave encouraged Elias and the other Christian men to have family prayer and devotions. This was significant because for thousands of years married Chambri couples had not cohabitated. The men usually slept in the spirit house while their wives slept in their own huts with the children.

There is an old Chambri belief that if men heard a woman's voice too much, they would turn into a termite. Women who intentionally violated the "cohabitation" law could be put to death. Needless to say, the law was taken very seriously. (A mediator would arrange conjugal visits when desired.)

The gospel brings about spiritual transformation in a culture. Among the Chambri, it was beautiful to see some of the changes in the area of marriage as Christianity gained a foothold.

One afternoon around sunset, Dave and Connie were sitting under their netted veranda looking out over Chambri Lake when they heard Elias and his wife laughing. That may seem like a small thing. But they had never heard any husband and wife laugh together on the island, so this was an historic moment. It was thrilling to see the Lord bringing about transformation in the Chambri culture as His word was beginning to permeate the area.

It seemed as though the Lord had used fiery, aggressive personalities such as Leo Wasi and me to kick down the doors for the entrance of the gospel. Then Dave Baker and Elias Sarin were following up with solid Bible teaching and discipleship of new believers. These men were significant co-workers, and the work could not have progressed without them. We recognized our different giftedness and roles in the mission. As Paul said so well, "I planted, Apollos watered, but God gave the growth."[46]

Gospel Seed

Some things are givens in the missionary experience, and one of those is demonic resistance. Producing faithful followers of Christ among peoples who are in the tight grip of a demonic stronghold is like trying to reason with a drunken man in a fist fight. It is fruitless, except by God's power and grace.

---

46 1 Corinthians 3:6

There seems to be a regular progression of events that occur when the Lord begins doing a transformative work among unreached peoples. After the initial spew of furious opposition, there tends to be a time of surface tranquility. However, the wise missionary recognizes that this is when the battle really begins. Outwardly, it often feels like a stagnant phase when nothing much is happening. But, this is when the Lord is doing His undercover work of preparing hearts of people for Himself. It is a work that only He can do.

During this preparatory period it may seem there are only glimpses of progress, but it is the missionaries' responsibility to persevere in prayer, continue teaching truth, and work on removing any needless cultural obstacles to faith. This is what it means to plant and water. And like a farmer, the pioneer church planter waits for the promised harvest.

As the year went on, a noticeable change began to occur among Chambri villagers. I had made it a top priority in my stateside travels to encourage American believers to pray fervently for the Lord to open Chambri hearts, and I was encouraged that many had pledged to pray and even fast for a spiritual breakthrough among this staunchly resistant tribe.

I often asked the Lord to lift the curtain of the spirit world a bit, so I could peek at what He was doing. Nevertheless, I knew the most crucial thing happening in this quiet phase was the fervent intercession of God's people. These precious pleadings were drawing the tribe to the brink of spiritual breakthrough. Unseen, a dramatic shift in the spiritual climate on Chambri Island was occurring that was entirely unexplainable, except by intercessory prayer!

Elias and his family were now living in Chambri, and he spent the majority of his time teaching the Bible to the small number of Chambri believers. In the evenings he debated spiritual questions with the tribal leaders in the *haus tambaran*. With this small group of believers, the spiritual battle lines were being drawn, and Chambri souls were literally perched on the line.

After years of incessant conflict, constant trickery and scheming of the enemy, a period of calm was settling over Chambri. This was a very welcome period of relative peace and rest. In August, I led a short-term mission team of twenty-seven people to Chambri Island. The focus of the trip was to use medical clinics to relieve some of the physical sufferings of the people and practically demonstrate the love of Christ. People thronged to the clinics from morning until night. In the evenings, the *Jesus* film was shown again and the gospel was explained. This was the first time we had been able to speak of Christ openly without having rocks and coconuts thrown at us.

Once there were new converts, the next step in my church planting strategy had always been to emphasize, from the very first moment of conversion, the privilege and responsibility that is ours to extend the gospel into other unreached regions. Even before the church was established in Chambri, I led Leo and the others on outreach patrols into nearby villages, some of which had been traditional enemies with the Chambri.

Typically, the initial research patrols were only exploratory in nature. While the doctors put together one-day medical clinics, I met with the village leaders. However, something unexpected happened as the team came ashore at Timbunmeri. We heard loud wailing as we approached. We discovered that the village was in mourning over a young woman who had died unexpectedly. The people were on edge because the village sorcerer had tried to appease the evil spirit they believed had murdered her.

Fear was rampant. Everyone was terrified that others would soon be killed. The mourning families sent me a message and asked me to speak with them. I opened the Word and encouraged them to put their faith in Christ who is greater than all the spirits that rule over and afflict them. "For all the gods of the peoples are worthless idols, but the Lord made the heavens."[47] From that text and others like it, I spoke of God as the one, true, sovereign, supreme God that rules as King over all of the gods of the nations. And this God has a Son!

No one turned to Christ in Timbunmeri, but seeds were being planted. I always tell our missionary teams "keep planting gospel seed, the seed knows what to do."

: : : : : :

Important relationships were developed in several villages on this trip. On the last day before returning to Chambri, the team canoed to the village of Paliagwe. We were wet, exhausted and disorganized after being in different villages every day for nearly a week. When we arrived we were invited into the guest house to rest.

Paliagwe was a religious village, dominated by syncretistic Catholicism. Although they believed in Jesus, they insisted that it was also necessary to worship and pray to a whole legion of saints and spirits, particularly the popular ancestral spirits and, of course, Mary the Mother of Jesus. They believed that salvation was most likely if they would simply add Jesus and Mary onto the list of deities they already worshipped.

After some private discussion, the village leaders asked me to speak in the open air to the people. Knowing their idolatrous leanings, I explained clearly that there is only one God and one mediator between God and men. Then I asked the crowd: "Who is the mediator?" They yelled out in unison, "Mother Mary, Mother Mary!"

---

47 Psalm 96:5

I shouted back, "No! The Virgin Mary didn't die on the cross as a ransom for all men. Jesus Christ is the one mediator, and there is salvation in no one else!"[48] Upon hearing this, one villager immediately jumped up and bumped his chest hard into my chest, raised his fists to my face, yelling and cursing the whole time.

If not for the medical team who was at that very moment tending to their sick, there may have been bloodshed in Paliagwe that day. The medical team assisted 800 people in four villages over the span of this five-day outreach, treating villagers with malaria, joint pains, skin fungi and pneumonia. They also pulled teeth, performed minor surgeries, distributed seventy pairs of eyeglasses and saved the life of a woman who would have died from an infection caused by a retained placenta.

Concurrently, the evangelistic members of our team preached the gospel to more than 1,500 people. Many seeds of the kingdom were planted throughout the Chambri Lakes region that summer. I hoped to have many more opportunities to reach these tribes more fully once the church was better established in Chambri.

48 Acts 4:12

Antonio; her death put into motion events leading up
to the power encounter

Chapter 9
Machete Bob

IN THE SUMMER OF 1995, I chartered two Missionary Aviation Fellowship airplanes to transport another mission team from
Wewak to Chambri Island. Thirty minutes after we arrived in
Kilimbit, a twenty-year old woman named Antonia, one of the
four believers on the island, died unexpectedly.

One of my team members was the last to speak with her before
she died. This was alarming to me because tribal people do not
believe in natural death. They believe when someone dies, particularly a younger person, someone else must be responsible for
that death. Obviously, since one of our team was the last to see
her alive, we would be a prime target of accusation.

In order to find out specifically who caused the death, the people
developed a ritual to determine who the culprit is. The ritual is
called *wokim mambu* (the shaking of the bamboo). Here is how it
works in Chambri:

The initiated men of the tribe meet at the *haus tambaran* or some
other specially designated place and begin dancing, chanting, yelling and making noise in an attempt to rouse the spirits. As this is
taking place a young man, usually a new initiate, holds a long bamboo pole in his hands, palms up and horizontal to the ground. He
dances with the pole until the spirits take control over it. He then
releases it once it starts to levitate. Eventually it bounces around

David and Elias (one of the Chambri pastors)

and points out the individual or clan who caused the death of the person. The identified person is sometimes killed in order to appease the spirits.

The Chambri openly boast how even their children can engage the spirits in rituals. For years, I had been hearing from them that "calling up the spirits" was easy for their sorcerers. I had no doubt that Satan was capable of moving a piece of bamboo and inciting the people to further bloodshed. This was nothing new. What was new was that the Chambri were about to be embroiled in a massive spiritual conflict that would affect all of the villages.

Antonia died on Saturday morning and was buried Saturday afternoon. Sunday evening it was time for the *wokim mambu* ritual.

"I want to go to the ceremony," I said to Elias.

"Absolutely not," Elias said. "Under no condition would it be appropriate for you to go. Don't even think of it."

"But Antonia was a Christian, and I don't like the thought of them attempting to 'call up' her spirit from the grave."[49]

"You being there won't help anything. It will just make things worse."

"Well, I'm going."

Although Elias was adamantly opposed, he finally gave in, knowing I wouldn't back down on this one. We engaged in a long time of prayer, asking for God to help us and show His power through

---

49 Divination and necromancy are ancestral cult practices that are explicitly forbidden by God (Deuteronomy 18:9-13).

us in some way. Then we walked toward the spot at the end of the grass airstrip where the ceremony was to take place. Nervous murmuring could be heard all around as we arrived: "What are they doing here?" "Who do they think they are? They must be the reason Antonia died. We must kill them once and for all."

The people were shocked that we had the audacity to show up at their private ceremony and sit down on a log to watch their private ceremony unfold. They were livid but allowed it, probably thinking the bamboo would quickly identify us as the cause for Antonia's death, which would give them the reason to kill us on the spot.

The Ritual

The sky was an eerie red color as the sun began to set. Tension hung thickly in the air as the villagers began making rapid smacking noises with their tongues. When the tongue smacking happened in unison it had an evil, darkness attached to it, much like the creepy, edge-of-the-seat music in a horror flick that warns of something bad about to happen. All we could do was sit quietly on the edge of a log and wait.

Two young males with scarred skin still swollen from their recent initiation "cuttings" got things started. One carefully held the six foot bamboo pole, while the other tapped on the far end of it with a human bone. The sound of the bone rapping on top of the hollow bamboo echoed loudly. This combined with the noise of the continued tongue clicking and the steady beat of kundu[50] drums made for quite an ominous atmosphere. The man with the human bone began chanting softly, inviting the spirit of Antonia to come into the bamboo and to point out the person guilty of her death.

50 Kundus are hand-held drums that are carved into an hour-glass shape. Hands beat rhythmically on the snake or monitor lizard skin that covers the opening on one end of the drum, which makes a beautiful thump thumping sound.

I got as close as possible to the men conducting the ritual so I could see and hear what was happening. As the men chanted for the spirit of Antonia to appear, I was provoked and shouted: "Antonia was a Christian, her spirit is in heaven."

My heart pulsated hard against my chest. Again I was compelled to yell sharply, in order to be heard above all of the noises of the ritual and the crowd of people: "Precious in the sight of the LORD is the death of his saints!"[51] "To be absent in the body is to be present with the Lord!"[52] Other verses crowded into my mind and flowed out of my heart and mouth as a rebuke to the spirit world and those that were its ambassadors.

"Antonia will not appear tonight; you are calling upon evil spirits to empower the bamboo, and I forbid them to come forward in the name of the Lord Jesus."

I shouted to God, asking that He hinder the evil spirits who would seek to take over control of the bamboo. It was an intense time of spirit warfare as the young sorcerers called upon their evil spirits, and I sought the favor of the one true God.

Finally, one of the men threw the bamboo down on the ground and with an irritated voice said, "The spirits won't come tonight."

"Why won't they come?" I called out. "I thought manipulating the spirits was so easy that even your children could do it. Why has the bamboo not moved? Could it be that our God is more powerful than yours?"

It was pitch dark. Nothing could be seen except for a few moving shadows in the moonlight. Suddenly, I heard what I thought were people running toward us. I yelled to my team, "Run!" As I looked around, I realized that Clay Jones, my good friend from Colorado, and I were the only ones left. The rest of the team was already halfway down the grass airstrip running toward camp!

---

51   Psalm 116:15
52   2 Corinthians 5:8

Ironically, it turned out we weren't being chased at all. The rustling noise was merely angry tribesmen gathering coconuts to throw at us. My team walked back to the gathering after realizing it was a false alarm. I encouraged them to keep praying.

Turning my attention back to the crowd, I noticed out of the corner of my eye a woman gyrating her body, dancing, swiveling provocatively and screaming loudly and passionately to the spirits.

"Come speak to us. Show us who killed Antonia. We worship you and will do as you direct. Antonia, come yourself. Show us, our dear one, who is responsible for your death?"

She was trying to levitate the bamboo pole by the power of the spirits, even though she stood thirty feet away from it.

This was the sorceress, Rosa. She was desperately trying to communicate with the spirit of Antonia or any other ancestral spirit that could guide the bamboo and identify who was responsible for the death. I continued yelling out Scripture that proclaimed the supremacy of God over all other spirits.

Then, another amazing thing happened. I had never done anything like this before and it was certainly not something I had planned in advance to say. I yelled out, "ROSA!"

Everyone, including Rosa, went silent. "Rosa," I said, "if you can get the spirits to move the bamboo, we will follow and worship your spirits, but if you can't do it, you need to follow and worship our great God."

Rosa, the sorceress who confronted David

I was stunned at my own words. Even as they tumbled out of my mouth, there was a strange kind of fear in my heart. Of course, I knew that my God was more powerful than the spirits but, if He didn't choose to prove it in that moment, all of us could be killed. Countless missionaries through the centuries had been killed for a lot less than what I was doing.

Rosa ratcheted up her desperate pleas to incite the spirits to action, while I continued yelling out prayers to God and rebukes in Jesus name against men and demons. Finally, Rosa gave up. A young man angrily shoved the bamboo into the doorway of a hut.

I gently taunted them, "Rosa can't do it. Send out someone stronger. You insult us by sending a woman. Send your most powerful man." But no one would step forward.

There were a few moments of silence. The Chambris are black people and I couldn't see them, but I could hear the crackling of leaves as people moved around hurriedly in the darkness. Suddenly, large coconuts began hitting the ground all around us. I yelled for my team to run again, and they scattered back toward camp. I remember looking around to see where my team was and I saw one of our young women, Emily Barefoot. She was wearing a long white dress. I looked around just in time to see her jump over a six-foot wide drainage ditch. All I could see was that white dress fluffing out like a parachute as she landed on the other side and sprinted down the airstrip towards camp..

An ear-shattering scream brought my attention back to the crowd. One of the young tribesmen who had started the ritual charged straight at me with his machete raised high over his head. He screamed at me, "*Yu Bin Bagarapim Kastam Bilong Tumbuna Bilong Mipela.*" (You have destroyed the ritual of our ancestors!)

His machete swung to the right and left over my head. I heard the *swoosh* again and again as the machete man kept taking swings.

I stepped backwards, trying to avoid getting slashed. The machete man swung again, this time left to right, again just missing my head. I took a few more backward steps. I saw the sharp machete poised over me and I turned quickly away to protect my head. But, the final blow never came.

When I looked around, I saw that another Chambri man had stepped in-between me and the machete man, preventing my death. I gulped a few deep breaths. God had delivered me from death once again.

The man who saved my life was named Casper. He did not believe in Jesus, but after he had witnessed the encounter between me and Rosa, he didn't want me to be killed on their island. Having witnessed the power of our God as superior to the power of the Chambri spirits, Casper was afraid of what this God would do to them if I was killed.

It was a tough but glorious night. I, along with eleven others, witnessed our great God publicly and powerfully rebuke the spirits that had ruled over the Chambri region for hundreds of years. How amazing that my life had been saved by the very people who had been trying to kill me! They intervened to save my life because, for the first time ever, they recognized the superiority of the one true God over their numerous tribal deities.

Still reeling from the events of the evening, I briefly wrote a single sentence in my journal: "The Lord gave us courage to aggressively oppose Rosa to her face." I know we would not have had the ability to do such a thing on our own. God had demonstrated His power in the gospel by disarming the demonic entities in Chambri. What a privilege to advance the Kingdom of God, thus crushing the gates of hell in a region where Satan had ruled, nearly unchallenged, for centuries.

The following morning, the machete man who had nearly killed me came with a peace offering of two betel nuts and an apology. He said, "I don't understand what happened last night, but I almost killed you!"

I replied, "I know what happened. God showed his dominance over the Chambri spirit world. You are controlled by evil spirits. But several times last night you saw that your ancestral spirits are far inferior to the power of our God. You need to repent and believe the gospel. Turn to the Lord and be saved."

Although Mambunambi, "Machete Bob," as I began to affectionately call him, did not turn to the Lord that day, he began following me wherever I went. When I showed the *Jesus* film, he was there to carry the generator and projector. When I went to other villages, he insisted that I use his canoe and boat motor. He became a valuable help to me in the gospel, even though he did not believe in Jesus himself. In time, he would become one of my best friends in Chambri.

A few years later I received a letter telling me that "Machete Bob" had become "Brother Bob" through faith in Jesus Christ.

"Machete" Bob (in rear, paddling David's team into the Chambri swamps

Chapter 10
A Big Surprise

IN THE SUMMER OF 1996, I chartered two more airplanes and returned to Chambri with another team. Some have joked that the biggest miracle was that I could recruit anyone at all to join me again after I was nearly decapitated in the region the year before.

This time, upon arrival in Chambri, something was noticeably different. The small group of believers who had regularly gathered to discuss the Bible was now much larger, eager and more energetic in their faith. They sang vibrantly and had a heightened interest in what they were studying. They were asking lots of questions and excitedly discussing passages. As I sat in those first gatherings, it became apparent to me that these people were no longer God-seekers. These men and women had become true God-followers!

Over the previous ten months, forty-nine Chambris had come to faith in Christ! Elias had purposely neglected to tell me this rather significant news. He wanted me to discover it on my own. It was a stunning realization that, for the first time ever in the history of the Chambri, a church was being established among them. Once I returned to Wewak, I wrote to my supporters:

"Since the day we first learned of the Chambri, fierce warfare has raged with the enemy for the soul of this tribe. Through riots, death threats, stoning with both rocks and

coconuts, face-to-face confrontations with angry sorcerers and a full array of physical and spiritual attacks, Christ
was still proclaimed . . . God has changed the spiritual
climate of the entire island. Those who once furiously
opposed us are now eager to hear the gospel. We are eye-
witnesses of this incredible outpouring of God's grace."

"I envision this picture of Satan in my mind: he is driven
out to the far edge of Chambri Island. He has one foot
on land and one foot in the swamp. The deceiver of souls
is being driven out of Chambri."

I had spent many evenings in the Kilimbit spirit house, but this
time was special because I was invited to talk specifically to the
village leaders about serious spiritual matters. For several hours we
talked back and forth and round and round. I took every slight
opening to weave in gospel applications. I reminded the men how
harshly I had been opposed by them when I first came to the island,
how they had beaten me up and threatened my life time and time
again. Ironically, this was most likely the reason they were giving
me an audience. I had earned their ears!

They had many questions and they didn't always like my answers.
Some answers stirred passionately negative responses. They were
listening, but clearly, not yet believing.

Two days later, a runner came to me with a message from a
young couple named Jon and Prisca,[53] asking if I could visit them
soon in Wombun. They had heard bits and pieces of the gospel
from the Chambri believers, but they wanted to hear the whole
story themselves. I loved telling them about Christ, the one and
only, all-sufficient sin-bearer for the entire world, the only way

---

53   Jon and Prisca's tribal names are *Sanapan* and *Wananpramp.*

and hope to be reconciled with God. They received the message with joy. Prisca's face lit up like an angel as she first experienced the joy of knowing that her sins were forever forgiven.

However, Wombun was the spiritual stronghold of the enemy in Chambri. The fiercest opposition and persecution had always come from that end of the island. An important part of understanding the gospel for Jon and Prisca was to recognize from the very first day of conversion that in following Christ there is a daily cross to carry.[54]

Even as I shared these hard truths, several Wombun men showed up and ordered me to leave immediately. I stood in the little window of the hut looking down at them in their blindness and ignorance. I began to pray out loud that God would have mercy and give them grace to believe in Jesus. This only made them angrier, and they soon started throwing rocks at the house. What foolishness!

I encouraged Jon and Prisca to be daring in following Jesus and to be ready to endure serious hardship for the Name. I urged them to be faithful witnesses of Christ by quickly and publicly being baptized. They agreed to walk to Kilimbit to meet me later that day.

When I left the village, several men threw coconuts at me, but two young men got close enough to actually whisper in my ear: "We're with you. We want to hear more about Jesus too."

Jon and Prisca didn't show up that afternoon and I was concerned that they had been hindered in some way. The problem was with Jon. He had lost heart and was afraid because of the threats and taunts of the Wombun villagers.

However, Prisca showed up the next morning to see me just as we were preparing to leave for Wewak. She was beautifully radiant with the joy of Christ in her, and she wanted to be baptized. What a great moment to have Elias baptize her in the Kilimbit bathing hole!

54   Matthew 10:3-39; Luke 9:21-27

My journal notation for that day mentions my belief that the Lord was going to use Prisca mightily in Wombun. I already had a sense that perhaps the Lord had chosen to give her the gift of special suffering for the gospel among her people.[55] My final journal entry regarding this trip to Chambri was a single sentence:

Last year we had five believers in Chambri and now Prisca makes fifty!

Storytelling in Changriman

The following summer, I visited the nearby village of Changriman. Overloaded with people and medicines, the canoes nearly capsized on the way across Chambri lake. The usual forty-minute canoe ride took more than two hours.

I was immediately invited into the village spirit house. After the usual introductions, the men asked me to tell them a story. This is a common request as Papua New Guineans are always curious about how we live in America. I agreed to tell them stories, but I wanted to hear theirs first. I asked the tribal elders to tell me about their original ancestor and how they had come to exist on this island in the middle of a remote swamp.

This was an important part of my strategy. Every people group has some kind of story that satisfies the need to know about their origins. By learning what people believe about their "creation story" and listening carefully to the mythologies and legends about their ancestral history, missionaries often gain insights[56] that provide a strategic starting point for the gospel. Tribal peoples often come to see Christ and the gospel as a fulfillment of their own ancestors' search for truth. Christ becomes not a new religion but the very fulfillment of the longing in the hearts of their own forefathers.

---

55 Philippians 1:27-30. Suffering is as much a gift from God as faith is. Both are mentioned in verse 29.
56 These cultural insights are sometimes called "redemptive analogies."

The Changriman village leaders began to tell me about *Kaipon*. I didn't get the story from one man; rather, they eagerly took turns talking, often interrupting each other, to relate different details of their history. I was told emphatically that Kaipon had somehow emerged out of a large stone. They couldn't explain exactly how this happened except to say that Kaipon had no earthly parents. The Changriman refer to this stone as "Kaipon's father." They went on and on with great detail about Kaipon and his friends and relatives. As the story line developed, they began describing a pillar-shaped tower built by their forefathers that extended high into the clouds.

The Changriman, like many unreached tribes, were a pre-literate society. They had no written language. What they knew of their past was a result of oral transference. In that moment, in that spirit house, late at night, deep in the New Guinea swamps, I sat in stunned silence as these tribal elders told me the biblical account of the "Tower of Babel."

I interrupted them with a question: "When did the first missionaries come into Changriman with the story of the one, true God?" They looked at me quizzically, not understanding how my question related to the story of the tower. They claimed that no missionaries had ever visited their village before.

I asked about their people who sometimes traveled back and forth to other villages along the Sepik River. Did they ever return to Changriman with stories about the tower that reached into the clouds? Once again, they said no. They insisted that this tale of the tower is a true report of the lives of their own people from "*bipo, bipo tru*"—from ages past.

After they convinced me the story of the tall tower had been orally transferred, from generation to generation through the centuries as families sat around the Changriman campfires, I had a question, "What happened to the tower?" They didn't seem to know. I was exhilarated by what was happening. I started rattling off questions, hardly waiting for answers before posing the next.

"Do you know why your people built the tower?"

"Do you know why there are so many different languages?"

"Do you understand why people are scattered all over the world and have different colors of skin?"

They didn't know the answers to the questions but were very eager to hear my explanations. This provided the perfect segue to share the Genesis account of the "tower" story:

> "The first man God created was Adam, but here in Changriman, he is known as Kaipon. You believe that Kaipon came out of a stone, but the truth is God formed him out of the dust of the ground. Before long, through Kaipon, sin entered the world. That sinful nature has been passed along to all of Kaipon's descendants, even until now. Kaipon's tribe became large and influential. At that time in history, there was only one group of people. They all spoke one language. They had one culture, one color of skin, and they lived in the same area of the world. Papa God told the people to scatter and populate the whole earth, but they disobeyed Him. Instead of scattering, they congregated in one place. They began to build a huge tower that was so tall that it seemed to disappear into the clouds."

They were shocked that I was able to provide important details that closed some of the gaps in their own story. I reminded them how they told me they didn't know why their ancestors had built the tower. I knew the reason and told them:

"They did it because they were arrogant. They wanted to make a great name for themselves. And they were able to accomplish a lot because they were a large group of people who shared a common culture and language. They thought that if they became a great enough people they could disobey and not go and populate the earth, as Papa God had told them to do. God saw the arrogance and disobedience of the people, and He was angry. To disrupt the unity of the people and their ability to work well together in constructing the tower, God confused their language, so they were no longer able to communicate. Then the Lord fragmented the one people into what are now thousands of people groups. In their confusion, the people wandered across the face of the earth and eventually settled down into scattered communities all over the world. As the generations have passed, people have developed thousands of different lifestyles, cultures, religions and philosophies which are now represented all over the world today. This explains why people have different skin colors, why they live in different places with radically different cultures, and why they now worship a whole variety of gods and spirits."[57]

The Changriman village leaders were shocked into silence. They spoke in awed whispers and cautiously asked questions, which gave opportunity for further elaboration, but mostly they just listened soberly. Those few hours were an incredible moment in which the powerful, yet peaceful presence of God was experienced by everyone in the hut. It was clear the Lord was doing His work in the hearts of these village leaders. To this point, I had been giv-

---

57   This is the story I told the Changriman leaders directly from Genesis 2:7; Genesis 3; Romans 5:12; 1:1-9; and Genesis 11:1-9.

ing spiritual truth through story without quoting directly from Scripture. But now, I picked up my Melanesian Bible and under the light from my flashlight I slowly, without commentary, read these words:

> "The God who made the world and everything in it is the Lord of heaven and earth . . . He himself gives everyone life and breath and everything else . . . From one man (Kaipon) he made all the nations, that they should inhabit the whole earth; and he marked out their appointed times in history and the boundaries of their lands. God did this so they would seek him and perhaps reach out for him and find him, though he is not far from any one of us.

> "We should not think that the divine being is like gold or silver or stone—an image made by man's design and skill. In the past God overlooked such ignorance, but now he commands all people everywhere to repent. For he has set a day when he will judge the world with justice by the man he has appointed. He has given proof of this by raising him from the dead."[58]

I explained with tears falling onto the pages of my Bible that is why I had come with this great news that provides answers and hope to the spiritual aspirations of their forefathers. It was no accident they were black Papua New Guineans living in Changriman village. It was not by chance they were alive today and not 100 years ago. And it was no coincidence that I was there that night speaking the very words of God to them.

---

58 Acts 17:26-31

"God did all of it. God made the world and all that is in it," I said. "Papa God is the one who gave you the ability to suck air into your lungs at this very moment. God determined in advance when you would be born, and He determined Changriman to be your home. You people here in Changriman are just a small people living in a remote village in the middle of a swamp. No one in the entire world knows about you. Even if they knew about you, they probably wouldn't care all that much. But God knows who you are. He made you. He put you here and He has sent me to tell you His story."

Unfortunately, the team couldn't stay in the village as long as we would have liked. We were on a quick tour hoping to visit as many villages as possible in order to assess the spiritual needs of each. For the benefit of the long-term work, we had to continue on our research patrol. However, before we left, I promised to return the following summer for a longer visit. I vowed to the Changriman people, "If I'm alive, I will be here next summer."

David Sitton, preaching in Changriman Village

Chapter 11
Promises Kept

"*KILL THE MAN WHO BROUGHT the rain! Kill him! Do you hear me?*" the sorcerer screamed as he pointed his bony finger at the inattentive carved bird, perched above the spirit house.

Elias, watching at a distance, just laughed at the foolish sorcerer. For weeks the people had been paying the witch doctor to intercede for them with the ancestral god of the birds to guarantee a successful collection of bird eggs even in the midst of a severe drought. Elias had been preaching and calling the people to acknowledge the one true God and submit to Him. "He alone created all things and He rules over His creation." He alone could provide the eggs. Elias then very unexpectedly blurted out, "You will not collect eggs because you refuse to give thanks to your creator."

As Elias and Dave Baker walked back to their huts after this encounter with the witch doctor, Dave asked Elias why he had said this. He answered, "I don't know, I was just really angry."

That very afternoon, dark clouds rolled in off the coast and rain began to fall. The water rose, covering the grassy lake bed and all the bird nests. The sorcerer had lost the battle between his bird god and Elias's Lord. He had been shamed before his people, so he was calling upon the spirit of the birds to kill Elias.

Although Elias had been threatened many times before, this seemed a little more significant. After all, this time the witch doctor was calling for his death.

The rain relieved the drought for a little while, but again the lake became dry. It was going to be a long summer. The drought became so severe that the fish were gone. Even the secondary food source, sago, was unavailable because there was no water to extract the sago powder from the palm trees. In fact, the drought was giving the enemy another platform to attack the Christians. The unbelieving tribesmen forced the Christians deep into the jungle to bathe and find drinking water, allowing them none of the limited quantity of water that could be found within the village. Fear of being beaten or ridiculed kept many young believers in their huts during this time.

One day the Bakers got an idea. They went to the Wewak city market and purchased seventy-five pounds of sago powder and had it flown out by an MAF charter to Elias and the Christians. The Christian families seized this as a great opportunity to love their enemies. They took the sago powder and distributed it not only among themselves but also to the non-Christians in their village. It was a great opportunity to bless those who had been cursing them.

About this time, I received a letter from Elias: "Brother, would you be willing to lead a team of Chambri believers on a patrol to some unreached pockets of swamp people on your next visit? We want to share the gospel with our neighbors."

Of course, this was an encouraging request to me, because Dave and I had trained Elias to think this way in the first place. I eagerly accepted the invitation to lead the team. But first, I was eager to fulfill my promise to visit Changriman.

The Mud-monsters

The 1997 team and I were shocked as we sat aboard a charter flight, looking down at miles and miles of sludge beneath us. After we landed on the Chambri grass airstrip, we were told the obvious. A severe drought had dried up Chambri Lake and canoe travel was impossible. Since the lake was dry, Elias assured me the Changri-man people would understand why I couldn't get to them as I had promised. "They know the lake is impassable," Elias said, "They would never expect you to come under these conditions."

"But, I promised them," I replied. "I gave them my word. We must at least try."

Seeing the resolve in my eyes, Elias shrugged his shoulders in resignation and went off to locate the smallest canoe he could find. The canoe he found was clearly made for a child, but it would work well to carry the essentials: water, food, Bibles and clothes. Dave and Connie stayed in Chambri with the rest of the mission team, while Elias, Tomas, two young Chambri girls and I started walking across the mud flats toward Changriman. We took turns pulling the canoe behind us with a rope.

The lake had completely evaporated except for a six-foot wide, eight-inch deep canal, obviously much too shallow for the weight of a canoe. My journal description went like this:

> There were many stretches where we waded through knee-deep mud. Several times I sank to the waist in quicksand. The Chambri girls jokingly called me "white horse!" For the first half-hour we laughed hilariously as we dug each other out of the paste. Before long, though, the jokes and laughter ceased. Our calves, thighs and lower backs began to cramp from the strenuous slogging. I remember complaining to the Lord: "It would be so

easy for you to just put a little water in the lake. Why all of this struggle?"

It took nine hours, completely unprotected from the 100 degree heat, to trudge through the sludge, before, like mud-monsters slithering out of a swamp, we crawled up onto the banks of Changriman village. The people stood on the banks of the mud lake in utter speechlessness. Some of the men even wept at the sight of us. They knew the condition of the lake and had already agreed among themselves that it would be impossible for me to keep my promise. They couldn't believe I was actually there.

After cleaning up, we went to meet with the men in the spirit house. These were the same men from the previous year that had told me the story of Kaipon and the tall tower. Once again, they listened intently and asked many questions. I began to realize that the difficulty of our struggle in getting across the lake had dramatically elevated in their minds the importance of the message we carried. Keeping a promise under such dire circumstances earned honor and the authority to speak directly.

At the conclusion of a few days of continuous conversations about the gospel, I was given a sheet of paper with a list of names on it. I was told, "These are the names of twelve men and our families. We want to follow your God!"

We were amazed at how the Lord had worked. The walk back to Chambri was somewhat easier, not only because the lake had a little more water in it, but because we were filled with such exhilaration at what the Lord had accomplished in the hearts of these men through our suffering.

On that trip I gained valuable insight into how God purposely uses suffering to advance the gospel more speedily. Slogging through the slop back to Chambri, I repented of my sinful, complaining heart, all the way back to camp.

Drawing a Line in the Sand

I led another large medical and outreach team back into the Chambri region in 1998. The plan was to complete a five-village campaign of medical clinics and nightly gospel preaching. We would start again in Changriman Village.

Late one night, I was invited by Brian, one of the older men, into the spirit house[59] to talk. He had become a good friend over the years, and we always exchanged gifts whenever I visited the village. As we reclined onto the platform, Brian went straight to the point: "I am an old man and I find it difficult to sleep at night. I wonder what will happen to me after I take my last breath and die. Where will I go? Will my body just rot and go back to dust? Will my spirit go to the place of the ancestors? Or will I cease to exist altogether? Help me, Brother David. Where will I go and what will happen to me when I die?"

It was a pleasure to share the comfort of the gospel with my old friend Brian.

Our next destination was the village of Mali. I had wanted to visit Mali for several years but had never yet made it there. Unbelievably, I had heard that no outsider had been to Mali since World War II when the Japanese occupied the area.

---

59 I've already described the interior decor of spirit houses. I will only mention here that they are built for intimate conversation and interaction. Men will often sit on the platforms that line the periphery of the hut during conversations, or they may even lie down, side by side, sometimes as many as twenty men lined up, either talking or snoozing together. Years ago, my good friend Leslie Minduwa, a national brother from PNG, visited me in the United States. I took him to the zoo. When we saw the fat orangutan gorillas lounging around eating bananas, Leslie remarked, "That looks like the spirit house in my village!"

It wasn't easy to get to the village. After a two-hour canoe ride, there was a twenty minute trek through swamp weeds, water lilies and hordes of mosquitoes and biting flies. However, once we reached the village, Mali seemed like an oasis to us. There were lots of coconuts, clean water, and it was actually a pleasant, though temporary refuge from the aggressive biting flies and mosquitoes.

Our medical team treated virtually every one of the 100 or so villagers in Mali, and then we talked with the men late into each night. Journal entry:

> These dear people would not be far from the kingdom
> if not for the lack of laborers.

Over the tough course of one week, our team of doctors treated more than 1000 people in six villages and supplied another 800 people with malarial medications. Most importantly, we freely gave the gospel to nearly 3000 people in these remote village outposts.

The Chambri fellowship had grown to about sixty believers, and it was a thrill to walk through villages shaking hands and happily hugging people who only a few years before were throwing rocks, if not swinging machetes, and threatening our lives.

It was exhilarating to see the Lord drawing Chambri men and women to Christ. Yet my concern was that many of the believers were simply using Jesus as additional "protection" from the power of spirits. They needed to understand that Jesus is not akin to a "rabbit's foot" that one hopes will obstruct bad luck or merely shield us from the fiery darts of Satan. The reason the Son of God appeared was to destroy the devil's work.[60] This is the consistent teaching of Scripture from beginning to end. [61]

Conversion can happen in a single moment of God's grace, but complete deliverance takes place over a longer period of time. I

60   1 John 3:8
61   Genesis 3:15; 2 Thessalonians 2:8; Hebrews 2:14; Revelation 20:10

didn't doubt that many of the Chambris were genuine believers in Christ. But they had difficulty in distinguishing between traditional tribal beliefs and their Christian faith. I was worried that some of them would view Christianity as a new and improved magic that could be used in conjunction with ancestral rites. They were naively coming to faith in Christ but were attempting to blend their new faith with animistic practices. For example, the Chambris would pray to God, but their prayers sometimes morphed into traditional chants that had been used to stir up slumbering spirits. They hadn't yet grasped that prayer to God is not a means of manipulating God to do things for them.

I compare the struggle of tribal people to "repent" of animism as similar to the difficulty that we in the West have in "repenting" of materialism. It isn't a simple matter of repenting from a single sin, but rather a re-orientation of one's entire way of thinking and living. This is the process of sanctification as the Holy Spirit teaches truth and transforms all of us steadily into the image of Christ..

For years I had freely gone in and out of the Chambri spirit houses, sometimes for social chats and napping with the boys, and at other times, to purposely engage them in serious conversation. An essential discussion is what I had in mind when I visited the spirit house near the end of summer, 1998. I needed to ensure that the believers rightly understood the gospel. Religious syncretism is a most serious matter! Light and darkness cannot co-exist; there can be no agreement between the temple of God (believers) and idols, neither can Christ and Belial share a fellowship meal![62]

Late one afternoon in the spirit house, I told the men the story of Elijah and his confrontation with the false prophets of Baal.[63] I purposely kept it brief, but left them with these words: "And

---

62 2 Corinthians 6:14-18; Deuteronomy 13:1-5 describes Gods anger has toward those that mix faith and idolatry.

63 1 Kings 18

Elijah came near to all the people and said: 'How long will you waver between two opinions? If the LORD is God, follow him; but if Baal is God, follow him.'"[64] I emphasized, "You can't have Jesus and Satan at the same time."

The next evening, I asked the men if they were afraid of death. "Yes, of course, we're terrified of death!" A spirited discussion ensued about the centuries-old fear of death that had been passed down to them from their ancestors.

Virtually every ritual, sacrifice and cultural taboo in animism is linked with their fear of the spirits and ultimately, their daily dread of death. Another question: "If you have your ancestors working for you, why are you so afraid of death? Won't they be able to save your soul?"

Stone cold silence was their only reply.

I challenged them with complete faith in Jesus alone, based upon His perfect life, all-sufficient blood sacrifice and the ultimate proof of eternal life through resurrection.

I said, "You have shown me some of your ancestral burial places. You continue to fear death because the ones you hope in are all rotting in their graves! You know in your hearts that your ancestors can't help you because they couldn't even help themselves. I'm trusting in the One that has already conquered death and the devil!" Some of the men stomped off in anger, others sat in silent thought. One thing was for sure; they were all listening.

---

64 1 Kings 18:21

Chapter 12
Spirit House Controversy

CHAMBRI ISLAND WAS BUZZING WITH excitement. The big day was fast approaching when the Chambri chiefs would officially dedicate a new *haus tambaran*. They had been working on this elaborate structure for several years. It was intricately designed, strongly built, and they were very proud of it.

I was surprised and disappointed when I learned that some of the Chambri believers were helping in the construction of the spirit house. I had overestimated the spiritual strength and maturity of the small fellowship of believers. I was shocked that some of the believers were actually planning to participate in the dedication ceremony. I sent a message to the three villages that I would be speaking on the grass airstrip the following night.

Several hundred Chambri gathered for the meeting. I told them the Genesis story about the Tower of Babel, how thousands of years ago the people had built a tall tower that reached into the sky. Building the tall house was an arrogant desire to "make a great name for themselves."

I pointed toward the new spirit house and said, "That is your tower to the sky! Your primary desire is to be known as a strong and significant tribe within the region. You only want to lift up your own name instead of giving glory to God."

I warned them to repent of arrogance and run to Christ to avoid the coming judgments of God. As I expected, the message was not well received. Sporadic muttering turned into loud shouting and threats. Two Chambri men charged at me with clenched fists and clubs. I was back-stepping with my hands and forearms cupped over the top of my head, while at the same time, trying to corral my team instead of having them scatter. As it turned out, it was just a minor scuffle, but they did communicate their displeasure.

More to the point of my own impatience with the dedication of the spirit house was the fact that it was now to be "ready for business." In fact, twenty-three young Chambri men were in the process of tribal initiation. These teens had already endured the sharp sticks and stones (razor blades) that tortuously cut their skin as well as the branding process of hot coals that singed their backs to create the elaborate designs and appearance of the "scaled" back of a crocodile.

Still covered in mud and traditional Chambri dress, these young boys were sequestered in the spirit house for their final tests. They were learning the sacred stories and traditions of the ancestors. They were taught about the intricate world of the spirits that only initiated men were privy to. In reality, tribal initiation was a systematic way of becoming willingly demon-possessed in order to have access to the knowledge and power of the spirits.

The Chambri men strutted around Kilimbit Village like clucking roosters, boasting how national politicians, government dignitaries and hundreds of people from all over the Sepik region were coming to see their beautiful, new *haus tambaran*. Even the Prime Minister himself, Sir Michael Somare, would be there for the ceremony.

Elias encouraged me to be patient. However, inwardly I seethed. I wrote in my journal about initiation rituals: *"What a blasphemy against our God!"* I was utterly distressed by it all. I was praying in the name of the Lord that he would rebuke Chambri for the sin of Babel, the pursuit of making a great name for themselves.

One day, during the dedication week, my team and I were walking past the new spirit house and several of the old men yelled to us an invitation to come inside and talk. This is the way the Chambri were; they would beat us up one day and want to chew betel nut with us the next.

Not to miss an opportunity with these men, I ducked into the short entry way into the hut. Once inside I reiterated, in a more informal fashion, some of the hard words about the ungodliness of the spirit house and the Chambri's prideful attempts at gaining further name recognition and praise from the surrounding villages.

One of the old men there that morning was Cletus.[65] I singled him out. "Hey Cletus, where are the other old men that used to hang out here in the spirit house?" I rattled off the names of a few men I knew had already died. "Where are those guys?"

Cletus was clearly uncomfortable with the question. But I persisted. Finally Cletus said, "David, you know those men have already died."

I replied, "Yes, I know they died, but where are they now?"

Some of the other men, along with Cletus replied, "We don't know."

I spoke to them about the afterlife, heaven and hell. I explained that salvation in Jesus Christ is the only way to heaven and that a denial of Christ would result in an eternal death and a fiery judgment that would never end.

Staring into the eyes of Cletus, I said, "Cletus, you're an old man! You won't live much longer. Are you going to run headfirst into hell too? Are you going to jump into the same eternal darkness as your ancestors?"

One of the old chiefs, Matyu, nervously mocked me. But Cletus was silent.

---

65   His tribal name was *Wanimbank*.

The next day Cletus came looking for me. "I couldn't sleep last night. I'm afraid of dying. I'm afraid of eternal fire and punishment."

I pointed him to faith in Jesus Christ, the One who carries all of the sin, sorrows and fears of those who believe. Cletus believed, and we rejoiced with him.

The spirit house was officially dedicated later that summer with a huge ceremony that was attended by hundreds of villagers from throughout the entire region, complete with all the food and fanfare that the special occasion warranted. However, I refused to participate.

The Ultimatum

The night before the team was to return to the United States, we went to the Chambri compound in Wewak to show the *Jesus* film one last time. Nearly 300 people showed up to watch. After the movie concluded with the ascension of Jesus, I began to preach. However, I never finished, because my old nemesis, Joaquim came sprinting out of the darkness yelling at me.

We stood face to face screaming at each other. Three other men joined Joaquim. The three distracted me by spitting betel nut juice at me, which gave Joaquim the opening to sucker-punch me from behind. The men were violently out of control, flailing punches and kicks left and right. I kept spinning in circles with my hands over my face to avoid the blows. By now, several more from the crowd had joined the ruckus.

Meaningful preaching was impossible with all the noise and confusion. Joaquim followed us to our truck shouting insults and threats. As I hurried the team into the back of the truck, Joaquim, with teeth blood-red from chewing betel nut, screamed at one of our young women: "If you ever come back here, we're going to drag you into the spirit house and line up to take turns raping you!"

Sarah Young, a young woman from New Jersey, not understanding the language and probably still in shock from all of the jostling around during the riot, looked straight into his eyes and smiled sweetly. Joaquim stomped off to the darkness, mystified by her unexpected reaction.

Later that evening as we gathered back at Dave and Connie's house, the team was somewhat rattled by all the opposition. But Dave and I were laughing and rejoicing! My journal entry for that night:

> The gospel of God's grace in Jesus has been forcefully proclaimed again among the Chambris. Our lives were in definite danger, and we could have been seriously injured, or even killed, except that so many Chambri came to our defense.

In fact, dozens of Chambri had stood up and physically protected us from further harm that day. Better than that, another dozen had surrounded us, quietly whispering to us their support. My newsletter that summer reported: "I admit that I'm becoming impatient with the old Chambri men. We had poured more love, prayer, time, effort and money into Chambri than any other tribe we've ever worked with. My message was getting sharper, 'Repent or perish!' Turn away from idolatry, burn the idols and live for Christ or the younger generation will burn them. Either become a part of it, or go die in the bush and get out of the way! The kingdom of God is overtaking Chambri. Either become a part of it, or go die in the bush and get out of the way."

Prisca

Chapter 13

Rape and Redemption

PRISCA SIRAMAKWI YAMBU WAS THE first convert from the Chambri village of Wombun. I had the privilege of leading her to the Lord several years prior, and at the time was concerned she would face severe opposition living for Christ as the only believer in the village. Nothing could have prepared me for what I was to learn about the extent of her suffering.

Two days before Prisca's mother died, she shared with Prisca some wonderful news: "There is a small amount of gold in your father's patrol box. Before you were even born, I put it aside for you. Go get the key out of my string bag and unlock the box. It's time for you to have this money. It's time for me to die now. Don't worry or cry. Take the money and leave this village. Hurry and return to our ancestral home."

Prisca held the small pieces of crumbling gold in her hand as her mother looked lovingly into her eyes and died a few moments later. Prisca was comforted by this unexpected provision from the Lord. She could now leave Wombun and begin a new life.

However, late that night, Prisca had a dream. In it, she saw the Wombun men chasing her down and beating her up with knives, tomahawks and stone axes. In the dream, Prisca saw the men disrespecting the Word of God and its messengers.

She also felt the Lord speaking to her. He said, "Don't be afraid. Don't cry. I'm not giving you a happy time just yet. I'm giving you a time of hardship and trial. Many are going to hurt you, but don't return their evil. They will hit you and your children with fists, rocks and harsh words. They will spit on you and break your bones. They will burn your house and run you out of this village to another place. But don't return evil to them. They will grind their teeth in anger at you, but they will not be able to kill you." She woke up from the dream, but didn't fully understand the nightmare that was about to begin.

I had just docked my canoe on the shore of Kilimbit Village late one night, when a messenger burst out of the jungle to meet me with an urgent note from Prisca: "They're raping me, brother, can you help me?"

Early the next morning, I hurried to Prisca's house; several miles walk away, not knowing what I would find. Upon my arrival in Wombun, I learned that it was true. Several men were making Prisca's life a living hell because of her strong witness for Christ. For months, she had been mocked, slapped around, and repeatedly raped by these village thugs.

Although I knew her life had been difficult, I was horrified to hear about the repeated beatings and brutal rapes. But I marveled at her determination to live for Christ no matter what she had to endure. Prisca had written me a letter some time earlier that demonstrated her strength and resolve, even in the midst of severe persecution:

> "When I believed in Jesus with all my heart, the people of Wombun began to fight against me. They were angry and didn't want me in the village anymore. They called me an evil spirit when I tried to tell them about Jesus. Even my husband Jon refused to believe. When I persisted

in telling the gospel, they burned our house down. Jon was angry and beat me with a tree stump.

"I am like a lost sheep of God, a no-name woman among my people; but God's grace is bigger. They burned my house down, but they couldn't kill my life. Jesus is my good Shepherd and I am safe within his fence."

Polygamy is a normal way of life in Papua New Guinea, so Prisca was not Jon's only wife, but she was his first. Jon had four wives and it was clear that Prisca was not his favorite. She was disliked by the other wives and disrespected by Jon's family and friends. When Prisca was pregnant with one of their children, Jon threatened to kill the baby while still in the womb if Prisca continued to bring trouble into their lives because of Jesus.

Prisca had been baptized when she believed in Christ two years earlier in Kilimbit Village, but she was eager to be baptized again. She insisted upon being baptized even more publicly because she wanted everyone to understand that, even through extreme hardship, she was a Jesus follower. I suggested we walk to another village where she wouldn't be so roughly ridiculed by her persecutors. But she rebuked me, saying, "You don't understand. I want to be baptized right here!" And she pointed to the nearest water right out in front of her hut, squarely in front of the whole village. She wanted to be baptized as a public declaration of her devotion to Jesus, and she wanted to do it in broad daylight, in plain view of her abusers.

As she requested, I baptized Prisca—a beautiful combination of humility, boldness and courage—right there in the village for all to see. Derisive laughter, taunts and disgusting insults were yelled at us as we walked back to Prisca's thatch hut. When it came time for me to leave, Prisca, face wet with tears, encouraged me, "It's okay, brother, you can go. The Lord is with me."

As I walked out of the village, the men threw coconuts at me and taunted, "When you leave, we'll get her again!"

And they did . . . time and time again.

Eventually, the men burned her house down again and even took the land that had belonged to her father and grandfather. Prisca, Jon and their children were forced to relocate to the uninhabited swamp island of Mansuat, where they struggled every day just to survive. Jon continued to beat Prisca because she insisted on following Christ so radically. Even the children received physical abuse at the hands of those that hated the gospel.

After being exiled to Mansuat, Prisca was forced to make long arduous trips across the lake by canoe. She didn't have a boat motor, so she and several of her children, paddled the canoe miles across the lake between Mansuat and Wombun. One trip on a late afternoon, the wind began to blow really hard and large waves were stirred up in the lake. The small canoe was tossed around so fiercely that it actually broke into two pieces. Prisca lost her two fishing nets and very nearly lost her children in the thunderstorm. She clung to them through the night on a small floating mound of kunai grass. At daylight she hand-paddled the damaged canoe back to Mansuat with her children in tow.

In a letter written afterwards and hand-delivered to me, Prisca wrote:

> "Here is my story of being with Jesus since my baptism. All that has happened in my life is God's plan. He chose me to be the 'truth mother'[66] for men and nations. God is good and precious. When I first told the gospel in Wombun Village, no one believed. I trust Jesus for all that I need. He is my perfect Father. He is sufficient for me.

66   She means by this "the carrier of good news."

I put all of my hope onto him. I hope you are happy to be chosen by our Father in heaven to be our encourager. Please keep helping me with your prayers."

I gave Prisca a notebook and encouraged her to begin writing down the story of her daily hardships. Prisca returned the notebook the next year with pages full of passionately handwritten testimony.

I had often wondered how Jon could allow Prisca to be continually humiliated by the Wombun rapists. I pleaded with him to stand up for Prisca when she was attacked, beaten up and raped. But he wouldn't do it. Fear melted his spine. Jon was a coward, and his wife paid the price. In fact, Prisca wondered if Jon was responsible for the many rapes she endured. In her journal she wrote down her thoughts in this regard: *"I swear to the true God of heaven! Why would my husband put me into the hand of another man, especially those that are enemies of God? My heart breaks at the thought of it."*

Rapes and physical abuse became a regular part of life for Prisca. Jon practically encouraged the rapes of his wife and offered no safety when she was physically harmed. Twice, Prisca paddled her small canoe to a district headquarters and filed rape charges against some of the men. One of the men even went to jail for six months. But once freed, the man was even more violent with her. Prisca wrote to me, "Jesus is my life, and he will help me. I trust him."

Prisca's Song

One day, Prisca invited me and my mission team to her reconstructed house in Wombun. She seated us in a big circle on the floor and announced that God had written her a letter. She called it a letter because she had written it down on paper. It was actually a song of love from her Heavenly Father. Prisca spoke very little English, but her song was nearly perfect. She stood up and began to sing a beautiful tribal-chanted love song as tears streamed down her face:

I love you Prisca
You are precious in my eyes
I created you through His death on the cross
You are mine
I love you
Accept my love
Let my love flow from you
Let it spill over to all you think
Don't be over-concerned with yourself
You are my responsibility
You are precious in my eyes
Love others because I love you
Look towards me and let go
Don't resist me, but surrender to my love
Rest in my love
I know what is best for you
I will shape you into what I want you to be
My will is perfect
My love is sufficient
Trust me
I love you

Prisca's life was a beautiful example of a recklessly offered up living sacrifice to her Savior.

Chapter 14
Apology and a New Beginning

A YEAR LATER, I WAS back in Chambri with another team that included some friends from a ministry called Surfing the Nations, from Honolulu. Upon arriving in Kilimbit with this new group, a messenger came to me with an invitation to the *haus tambaran* for an important meeting. I had no idea what the Chambris were planning this time.

As the team walked toward the spirit house, the men started to beat on the garamut drums and we could see the outdoor grass decorations swaying, as the men swatted them with sticks from the inside. This gave the large hut a ghostly look as though the entire spirit house was dancing. When we got inside, we saw the men dressed in full tribal regalia with brightly painted faces. They were laughing, blowing flutes and beating on the drums.

I soon discovered this was an "apology ceremony" for one of the past riots when some of our team had been beaten up. The men of Chambri had been concerned about the uprisings and riots that had been directed toward us and they wanted to make a formal apology. They stood in a long line to welcome each one of us and put necklaces around our necks. Several leaders made long speeches of respect and appreciation for my repeated visits to Chambri over the years.

The Chambri men who had led attacks against us in the past began stepping forward one by one and presenting clumps of

David Sitton, preaching in Chambri
(using the story of Saddam Hussein and 9/11
to preach the gospel)

betel nut (symbols of peace making) to us. As we accepted the gifts, the Chambri understood this to mean that we were accepting their apology. As only God can orchestrate, the guys from Hawaii had brought necklaces that we were able to use to reciprocate the Chambri gifts. It was a special time of reconciliation and friendship.

After the celebration and apology ceremony, the men began to ask questions. It was now February 2002 and over the previous decades, western influence had been creeping into Chambri. The men were more cognizant of what was happening outside their island. In fact, they had heard about the September 11 attack on America and were terrified that World War III and the end of the world were near. This widespread fear provided new opportunities for preaching Christ.

The men in the spirit house asked me, "David, tell us about that bastard,[67] Saddam Hussein. Is this the beginning of the end for us all?"

I shared what Jesus said when people had asked him a similar question many years before. He said, "You will hear of wars and rumors of war. . . nation will rise against nation and kingdom against kingdom, and there will be famines and earthquakes . . .

---

67   This is actually the word they used. It came out sounding like "bastad." This isn't a traditional Melanesian word, but in so many situations, the people learn English words and simply add them to the Melanesian vocabulary. This is a strong word they use in order to make their feelings known.

All of these are but the beginning of the birth pains"[68] and the beginning of the end time.

I added, "When I hear about Saddam Hussein and men like Usama Bin Laden, it makes me laugh, because it reminds me that King Jesus is about to return for his people. The return of Jesus is nearer now than when I was here last year. I'm ready to go. But, for those of you who will not follow Christ . . . yes . . . it will be the end for you all! Eternal destruction is coming soon for those that reject Christ."

I continued, "Yes. The end is near. And you need to run for your lives and try to save yourselves, because you have rejected your only hope of salvation that we offered you for all of these years. You have repeatedly beaten us up, burned our houses down, raped our women and tried to kill us. Run and try to save yourselves, because you have rejected Christ who is your only hope for now and forever after death. OR you can repent and turn to Christ."

The men had prepared a huge meal to eat with us in the spirit house, but after hearing this message, they thought it was too important to limit it to only the men of the village. One of the chiefs suggested that they move all of the food over to another hut so their women could eat the reconciliation meal with us.

After everyone had finished eating, one of the men stood up and said, "Brother David, please tell our women what you told us about that evil man, Saddam Hussein." I related the story of things that Saddam Hussein had

Chambri believer (Nick), studying the Bible (now with the Lord)

Chambri man in a tribal singsing

done to his own people and proceeded from there to explain the way of salvation through faith in Christ to all who would believe.

Later that evening, I was getting ready for bed in the hut of a Christian brother named, Bonifas[69] when two young men from Wombun arrived unexpectedly. The two men got right to the point. "Your words cut our hearts and we want to follow King Jesus." They repented and believed. I talked with them for a long while, telling them many stories from the Scriptures.

It was late at night when I told them the story of the Ethiopian in Acts 8. They were intrigued by the idea that this was a black man that believed in Jesus. One of them said, "What about us? We want to be baptized." I said, "There's water right out there in the lake. You can be baptized if you repent and believe in Christ." Without hesitation they said, "Let's do it!"

---

69   Bonifas' tribal name is Tunginduma.

Martina,[70] the wife of Bonifas, who was sitting in another room in the hut listening to the conversation, yelled out loudly, "What about me? I believe in Jesus, too!" I yelled back into the darkness, "You can be baptized too, if you believe in Jesus!"

It was late at night and both rain and mosquitoes were out in force. Still a large group of Chambris followed us down to the edge of the lake to watch the baptisms. It was a wonderful time of rejoicing over incredible grace that had reclaimed two more lost sheep of the jungle.

Chambri man taking a cigarette break from a tribal celebration

The next day, as we were preparing to depart, the four chiefs of the tribe told us, "From this moment on, you and your message are welcome in all of the Chambri Villages."

They were true to their word. There has never again been overt opposition toward me or any of our teams. As I was stepping into the canoe to leave, one of my staunchest enemies hugged me. With tears in his eyes, he said: "When you leave us, you are taking our hearts with you!"

---

70 Martina's tribal name is *Meragvnianp.*

Several Years Later

When I arrived at the Sepik River outpost of Pagwi in February of 2007, Lawrence Kamol,[71] a longtime hostile opponent, wanted to talk to me. Lawrence had instigated riots against us in the past, burned down Leo Wasi's house in Wewak, and once spat a big wad of betel nut juice into my face. Lawrence was also suspect in some of the most violent crimes against Chambri believers, including, possibly, some of the rapes of Prisca. I was surprised to learn that, since I had seen him last, Lawrence had become an enthusiastic follower of Christ.

He told me, "I believe in Jesus and I want to get baptized in Wewak."

"If you're serious, you know where I'm staying," I said. "Come by in the morning and we'll talk about it."

Surprisingly, Lawrence knocked on the door early the following morning in Wewak. A young man with whom he had been sharing the gospel accompanied him. I began telling them the gospel again in an attempt to find out how much of it they understood. Both men believed, and I baptized them that morning in the ocean next to the Windjammer Hotel.

After we all changed into dry clothing, Lawrence told me to wait for him in the Windjammer Restaurant because he was going to arrange a vehicle for us to use while we were in town. He assured me that he would return within an hour. However, he finally returned four hours later, with a huge grin on his face. I knew he was up to something.

Lawrence apologized for being so late and explained he had gotten held up at the Chambri compound because he was sharing the gospel with four of the influential Chambri chiefs. He said, "They all believe in Jesus and want to be baptized right now!"

---

71   Lawrence's tribal name is Pisas.

Henri Wapi[72] was the spokesman for the chiefs. He was nearly blind and wore big, thick black glasses. What was left of his hair was completely gray, and he always carried a walking stick. Henri leaned forward on a wobbly stool to get closer to me, talking excitedly the whole time: "Brother David? Have you ever heard of Jonah?"

"Yes, Henri," I replied. "I am the one who told you about Jonah."

Henri Wapi. One of the four converted chiefs. He told David – "I never beat you up, so you have to baptize me first!"

Henri said, "I'm like Jonah. God told him to go to Nineveh. But he disobeyed the Word of God. And God baptized him in the belly of a big fish. But the fish vomited him out on the beach. Jonah got up and went to Nineveh. I'm like Jonah. I've disobeyed God. But now I believe in Jesus. I want to be baptized and go to Nineveh."

He then said, "Brother David? Have you ever heard of Lazarus?"

"Yes, Henri. I'm the one that told you the story of Lazarus."

"I'm like Lazarus," Henri said. "I was dead and stinking in my sin! But God has given me new life. I want to go get washed in the water."

Henri added with a big grin, "Brother David. You know that I was never one of the ones that beat you up, so I get to be baptized first!"

The four chiefs went on to tell me their stories and how the desire of their hearts had changed: "All of our lives we have followed the ways of our ancestors. We were stupid men, men without any light or knowledge about God. We were ignorant to follow after them and to lead our people in the ways of darkness and fear.

72 Henri's tribal name is Kubia.

We believe in Jesus now. We want to use all of our remaining days to lead our people in the ways of God. Baptize us now so we can begin our new life with Jesus."

My good friend and Vice-President of *To Every Tribe*, Rod Conner had the honor of baptizing the four chiefs, along with Lawrence's wife, in the ocean, next to the Windjammer Hotel.

My journal entry for that was spirited:

> I've known these four chiefs for nearly twenty years. They've heard the gospel many times and rejected it. Some of them were hostile opponents toward us. But in those moments that they were baptized, I saw happy faces and genuine joy. They were old men in their seventies, but they were bouncing around and giggling like children.

Four converted Chiefs!

Part 2

STATESIDE

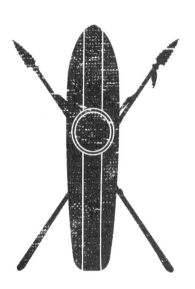

Chapter 15
Radical Redirection
Why Aren't You Living in PNG?

As mentioned earlier, in 1990 Tommi, our three kids and I were on furlough in Corpus Christi preparing for our return to Papua New Guinea. We were set for departure when we suddenly learned that our missionary visas would not be renewed. No visas—no permanent return to PNG.

I immediately returned to PNG on a tourist visa in order to find a way to get back into the country to live. Every door was slammed shut and locked. As it became clear that we couldn't return to PNG, this reality plunged me into severe depression. I was thirty-three years old and had been a missionary since I was twenty. Being a pioneer church planter was all that I had ever known as an adult. I had determined to do nothing else, but to live my whole life in pursuit of unreached tribes in PNG for the gospel.

I identified with how the Apostle Paul must have felt when the Holy Spirit denied him entrance into the province of Asia.[73] He then tried to enter Bithynia, but again the Holy Spirit would not allow it. But Paul pressed on, traveling through Mysia to Troas. That is where he received, through a vision, his next missionary assignment.

Since we were unable to return to PNG, Tommi and I decided to load up our three young children along with our few stateside belongings, and head to Pasadena, California to work with the U.S. Center for World Mission (USCWM).

U.S. Center for World Mission

Ralph and Roberta Winter, former missionaries in Guatemala, founded the U. S. Center for World Mission in 1976 after realizing that even if believers shared the gospel with every person in their culture, roughly half the people in the world would remain beyond the reach of the gospel because of cultural and linguistic barriers. Dr. Winter is the primary person who began to view the world ethno-linguistically. He coined the phrase "unreached peoples" and established the USCWM as a vehicle to champion the cause of "unreached peoples" around the world. "A church for every people" became the slogan of the USCWM and has remained at the heart of its vision for more than 35 years.

We had heard of the USCWM, but they had not heard of us. Furthermore, no one there even knew we were coming; we just showed up. Through some missionary friends, Tommi was able to make contact with the Providence Mission Home and make arrangements for a place to live in one of their two apartment buildings. Interestingly, as the manager of the apartments showed us into our new housing, she asked Tommi if she would like to manage the apartments, as the manager was planning to return with her family to the mission field! Tommi accepted, we received free rent, and Tommi entered one of the most enjoyable periods of her own ministry as the job was largely one of service and hospitality to a host of new missionaries constantly coming and going through their own ministry transitions.

Monday morning after we settled into our apartment, I put on my best clothes, walked into the main office of the USCWM, and introduced myself to one of the secretaries, Jody Van Loon. She didn't seem to think it strange that we had arrived from Texas un-announced. When I explained that we were missionaries who had been working with unreached tribes in PNG, her eyes brightened and she said, "You know, we've been praying that the Lord would send someone to work in the Institute of Tribal Studies (ITS) here on the campus."

She excused herself to make a phone call to Don Richardson, who had started the ITS a few years earlier. Don and Carol Richardson had been missionaries in Irian Jaya, New Guinea in the early 1960's and were then based in California. He began the ITS as a research institute in an effort to locate and identify the remaining unreached tribal peoples around the world.

Within days, I had met with Don and set up an office on the USCWM campus as the Director of the Institute. However, I was the only one in the office because the missionary who had preceded me had returned to the field!

Everyone we met seemed to be returning to the field. Returning to the field was my plan, as well, and I made several trips back and forth to PNG seeking to find a permanent way back into the country. Evidently the Lord had other plans for us, but they didn't fit very comfortably into my "vision" of ministry. I was completely downcast over our inability to return to PNG and endured several years of grueling depression. It was the unrelenting sadness of soul that some have called, the "dark night of the soul."[74]

I directed the Institute of Tribal Studies and Tommi managed the Providence Mission Home (PMH) in Pasadena, from 1990-1993. PMH is a wonderful ministry that was founded by Jacques and Mercedes Gribble specifically to assist furloughing missionaries with affordable, short-term housing. Our time in Pasadena was a great experience for us. The Lord brought many people into our

---

74   The phrase "dark night of the soul" originated with St. John of the Cross, a 16th Century Roman Catholic mystic.

lives, such as Ralph Winter and Don Richardson, who would serve us well in our next transition.

A Prophetic Word

I was increasingly restless in California and still hadn't accepted that the Lord would not allow us to return to PNG. If we were destined to be stateside, I reasoned, we should at least return to Texas and base our ministry closer to our families.

One night, I called my pastor, Jackson Boyett. As I described our desire to return to Texas, he became excited about it. Though I didn't realize it at the moment, this was one of those times when God was guiding us in a specific direction, and we were compelled to follow. As we talked, the Lord began to give me words, through Jackson's mouth, that we now know to be prophetic. The words burned into my heart, and, even now, I can recite them nearly verbatim.

"Brother, this (visas denied) is from God. What if the Lord wants to use your church planting experience on both sides of the ocean? Go ahead and return to PNG every year and continue your ministry through short-term trips, but also use that experience to recruit and train others for mission. The great need of the hour is for more missionaries, but not just big numbers, we need the right kind of missionaries. And how are we going to get the right kind of missionaries, if some of the right kind don't come home to train them?"

Jackson concluded, "Brother, what if the Lord brings you ten, or twenty, or fifty, or hundreds of missionaries who you can train and send around the world? They will do far more collectively to advance the gospel than you could ever do as one missionary family living in an isolated jungle village in PNG!"

This 'Word' was not agreeable to me, nor did I receive it immediately. To me, in that moment, it was "pathetic" rather than "prophetic." I did all I could to rebuke this "word" and "cast it out" in Jesus name! I was still unwavering in my desire to return to PNG and resume our full-time church planting ministry. However, I couldn't argue with the power of Jackson's words, and I stored them up in my heart as the seed of a new dream began to take root.

When we announced to our families that we were returning to Texas, they were overjoyed about our being nearby for the first time in our married lives. Our precise location was determined when Tommi's grandparents, Leo and Alene Moses had given us a long standing offer of an acre of their farmland in order to build a home, should we ever decide to relocate to Los Fresnos. Tommi's brother and sister-in-law, Mike and Kathy Moses, were home contractors. They eagerly built a home for us, at cost, often working through long nights and weekends, following long days of work on their other construction projects. There is no way we would ever have acquired a home like the one we have if it had not been for the graciousness of Tommi's family. We moved into our new home in Los Fresnos, on the southern tip of Texas near Brownsville, in 1994. Sadly, Tommi's grandfather died from cancer shortly before we were able to make the move back to Texas.

Missionary Mandate to Move On

I've never been much interested in carrying the gospel to places where the Church is already well established; I prefer to plant gospel seed in unsown fields. And, incredibly, even after 2,000 years of Christian history, there are still many unsown fields—some not far from home—where people have not heard a meaningful explanation of the gospel.

Living in Texas didn't ease the ache in my heart for Papua New Guinea. However, now living just fifteen minutes from the Mexican border city of Matamoras, I was intrigued by the mission opportunities that might present themselves there and wondered if there might be unreached people groups[75] in Mexico.

I am intrigued by something Paul said in Romans which has greatly affected the way I think about the remaining task of mission.[76] Surrounded by unevangelized masses, he explains that he is leaving the region from "Jerusalem all the way around to Illyricum (Albania)" because his aim is to preach the gospel, not where Christ is already named. Paul justifies his departure by quoting Isaiah, "Those who have never been told of him will see, and those who have never heard will understand."[77]

"There is no more place for me to work in these regions," Paul said, so he turned his attention to Spain which he considered to be the "uttermost" region where Christ was still not known. Is it true that there was really "no more work for him" in this huge geographic region? Certainly there were lost people all over that massive swath of territory that still needed to be evangelized. But for Paul, the pioneer church planter, he was compelled to move on to new areas where the gospel was not yet established at all. Once churches were strategically started in a particular field, Paul considered his job there as completed, and he focused his efforts on the more remote places where there was still no access to Christ and the gospel.

Paul was not implying by his departure that there was no more need for evangelization "from Jerusalem to Illyricum." He was simply making the point that this wide territory was now sufficiently

---

75   Donald McGavran, one of the foremost missiologists of the last 100 years defined unreached peoples as those who are "socially isolated away from gospel witness." Other definitions are more specific to say people are considered unreached if there is "no credible witness for the gospel within the host peoples language and culture (socio-linguistic ethnicity)."

76   Romans 15:17-25

77   Isaiah 52:15

reached so the remaining work of evangelism could be done by local believers in the churches he had established.

My understanding of Romans 15 leads me to argue that the natural progression for the gospel among unreached people groups is: unreached, reached, reaching.

1. Unreached Peoples are those among whom Christ has not been named; there are no self-reliant churches and *no meaningful access* to Christ and the gospel among them.

2. Reached Peoples are those ethnicities where Christ is now known; the gospel has been explained, some are converted, leaders are being trained, and a small fellowship of believers is being established. They are in process of becoming a "reached" people group. The crossover point from unreached to reached is when there are enough indigenous believers, within a strong enough national congregation, to complete the task of evangelization of their own people.[78] At this point, missiologists consider them to be "reached." A "reached" people is one where Christ and the gospel are now embraced, the church is firmly planted, the gospel is culturally and linguistically accessible to them, and the responsibility to evangelize the remaining unsaved within their ethnicity falls to the local believers.

3. Reaching Peoples are those that, with their own national manpower and local resources, are finishing the job of evangelization and the cross-cultural sending of indigenous

---

78 A vital distinction must be made between evangelism and mission. Both are critically necessary but they are different. Evangelism is sharing Christ and the gospel within one's own language and cultural environment. Mission is when one does evangelism and church planting cross-culturally. It is not technically correct to say "I am a missionary here at home" unless one is involved in evangelism among segments of society stateside that still do not have access to the gospel, such as Muslim or Hindu people groups. If we are not careful to retain the distinction between evangelism and mission, the category of the cross-cultural, language-learning, always-going-forward missionary is lost.

missionaries themselves. By this time, the church planting missionary should have long moved to other unreached places to repeat the church planting process.

With this understanding of mission, I turned my attention to the vast and widely divergent country and cultures of Mexico.

Unreached People Groups—in Mexico

One of the most celebrated symbols in Mexico is the "Virgin of Guadalupe" also called the "Virgin of Tepeyac" and "Our Lady of Guadalupe"—all names for the Virgin Mary.

The earliest Roman Catholic missionaries arrived in Mexico in 1523 to begin their religious conquest of Mexico. An Aztec Indian peasant named *Juan Diego* was among the first converts. On a chilly morning, December 9, 1531, Juan Diego walked across Tepeyac Hill to attend mass. It is said that he was brought to a sudden halt by a blinding light and the sound of heavenly music. Standing before him, in an astounding vision, was a beautiful young, dark-skinned woman. She called him "my son" and declared herself to be the Virgin Mary, Mother of Jesus. She told Juan Diego of her desire to see a church built on Tepeyac Hill and instructed him to relay the message to Bishop Juan de Zumarraga.

It wasn't easy for the lowly Indian to get an audience with the prominent bishop, but Juan Diego persisted in his attempts to see the bishop and finally succeeded. Bishop Zumarraga was incredulous when he heard Juan Diego's story of the apparition and demanded proof. Confused and fearful, Juan Diego avoided Tepeyac for several days. However, on December 12, the Virgin materialized before him a second time and he told her of the bishop's insistence for proof of the visitation. The Virgin directed him to pick some blossoms from Tepeyac Hill and present them to the bishop. When he did so, to the amazement of everyone, a perfect image of La Virgen Morena (the Dark-skinned Virgin) was miraculously emblazoned upon Juan Diego's jacket.[79] Very quickly, Bishop Zumarraga ordered a small church to be constructed on Tepeyac Hill.

The pertinent point as it relates to the question of unreached peoples in Mexico is that the Virgin's appearance on Tepeyac Hill is the exact spot where an Aztec temple had once stood. The temple was dedicated to Tonatzin (earth goddess, mother of the gods and protectress of humanity) and extreme measures were taken, including human sacrifice, to appease her. Tonatzin had a large and devout following, and the Indians felt threatened by Tonatzin when the temple was destroyed by order of Bishop Zumarraga. However, the construction of a Catholic chapel on this site eased the fears of the Indians and was a means of fusing the equally idolatrous Aztec and Catholic religions.

Religious syncretism, as described in the story of Juan Diego, is commonplace throughout Mexico but even more particularly within the states of Chiapas, Guerrero and Oaxaca.

Operation World, in its helpful overview of Mexico, states that there are at least 298 languages spoken in Mexico. A COMIMEX[80] statistical report is even more specific, citing 296 people groups, at least 26 of which have no viable gospel witness. Another 104 of these peoples are comprised of just a handful of believers with fledgling congregations in their villages. At least, another 12 areas are listed as "inadequately researched."[81] The Joshua Project lists thirteen Mixteco, Tlapaneco, Zapoteco, Popoloca and Nahuatl

---

79 The story of the Virgin of Guadalupe's appearance to Juan Diego is adapted from my book, *To Every Tribe with Jesus: Understanding and Reaching Tribal Peoples for Christ* (Grace and Truth Books, 2005) pages 81-82.

80 COMIMEX is an evangelical Christian organization whose vision is to create and facilitate cooperation, through strategic alliances between the different organizations and mission movements serving in Latin America.

81 Patrick Johnstone and Jason Mandryk. *Operation World,* 21st Century Edition (IMB, 2001), page 439.

people groups in Mexico.[82] My own experience, traveling through many remote regions of Southern Mexico, leads me to believe that even these figures are understated. One will drive day after day, through town after town of conservative Catholic communities where Catholicism reigns. But off-the-beaten-path peoples are both neglected and insufficiently researched, and the experience of missionaries is frequently hostility when the gospel is presented in these villages.

My good friend Bob Sundberg, with Arm of the Lord Ministry, told me a few years ago that he knows of 65 unreached indigenous peoples in the state of Oaxaca alone. These are almost completely untouched with the gospel, and many of these people groups don't even speak Spanish.

A large proportion of this "Ameri-Indian"[83] population, though baptized as Catholic, still adhere to many pre-conquest religious practices. "Catholic in name, pagan in practice" is the norm throughout Mexico, with only small pockets of vigorous evangelical expansions of the gospel.

In the summer of 2002, Bob Sundberg led a Suburban full of *To Every Tribe* missionaries on a trip into the high mountains of northwestern Oaxaca. Four-wheel drive vehicles are a necessity to access these villages, and even then, there is no guarantee of successful passage through and around the dangerously narrow and muddy mountain trails.

I will never forget standing in the cold wind on the high point of the mountain range overlooking an unreached indigenous people group of more than 25,000 inhabitants living in more than thirteen villages. At that time, there was only one known believer from among them. It was both an exhilarating and excruciating

---

82 http://www.joshuaproject.net/countries.php?rog3=MX (click Mexico map and scroll down)

83 The contraction Ameri + Indian refers to the native peoples living in North or South America before the arrival of Europeans.

experience. Exhilarating because we knew Jesus Christ and had in our possession the gospel that brings eternal life to all those who will believe, but excruciating because we didn't have the slightest idea how to contextualize the gospel message into their complex culture. This people group doesn't speak Spanish, and we didn't know a single word of their Mixteco dialect. However, we made a commitment that day that we would see to it, over the long haul of our lives, to do whatever is required so that the "knowledge of the glory of the Lord" will cover those distant mountains, even "as the water covers the sea."[84]

This is an extremely dangerous area. The people are very suspicious of outsiders because their primary cash crops include the cannabis plant and coca trees from which marijuana and cocaine is extracted. This particular people group has already killed one missionary that tried to enter their villages with the gospel. A Mexican brother from a neighboring village attempted to share the gospel here, but was chased out of the area with shotguns. He was later tracked down by some of the men of "X" village. He was able to escape, but his wife was not. Her throat was violently slashed from ear to ear and she died in the arms of one of her children.

We were not warmly received on our first short ventures into this area. The people glared with hostility towards us and rejected our greetings. The women simply turned away, refusing to even look at us as we walked or drove through their villages. They are an animistic indigenous tribe that continues, among many other things, to regularly slaughter chickens as offerings for healing and goats on an annual day of sacrifice to St. Mark, god of the rain.

I recorded the trip in my journal upon my return from the southern Mexico interior:

---

84 Habakkuk 2:14.

And so we returned to South Texas just a few hours ago. We are rejoicing in how the Lord used us a little for his glory among the "X" people. It is so thrilling to walk and pray and drive through those mountains and villages, to go face-to-face in hand-to-hand combat against the enemy of souls and to bind the devil and his minions in the mighty Name of Christ –and to hinder his evil intent for this nation.[85]

Since that initial journey into the state of Oaxaca, *To Every Tribe* has made countless short-term trips to this mountainous region as teams have provided much needed dental and medical care. After a few years of "earning the right to be heard" and the providential invitation by a village leader, To Every Tribe launched the first church planting team to live among this remote, resistant and unreached people group on September 1, 2010. There are many more unreached peoples in the interior parts of Mexico and the southwestern coastal areas who still need a clear presentation of the gospel. The Lord is preparing To Every Tribe missionaries-in-training through the Center For Pioneer Church Planting to be ready to, as my mentor Joe Cannon used to say, "go and get some of them for Jesus!"

---

85   Journal entry. (David Sitton, July, 2002).

Chapter 16
To Every Tribe
Short-term Missions into Northern Mexico

MATAMORAS IS A HUGE BORDER city of nearly 500,000 people who share the Rio Grande River with Brownsville, Texas. The vast majority of people live in poverty-stricken squatter settlements throughout the city.

We began making short-term mission trips across the border into Matamoras during the 1990's, simply learning how to get around in Mexico. I made contacts with two orphanages and delivered second-hand clothing, toys and food to the children. We also arranged minor construction projects, conducted medical clinics, Vacation Bible Schools, handed out tracts and Bibles, and preached the gospel through translators. These short-term ministries were a great training ground for us.

Before long, though, literally hundreds of people from our supporting churches around the country wanted to work with us on these one-week, cross-cultural "exposure" trips. Our staff, in those days, was only Tommi and me. We did it all, overseeing every detail from the recruitment, purchasing of food, water and ministry supplies, endless airport runs, arranging team housing, orientation, transportation across the border, organizing the ministry days, debriefing, clean-up and a final physical collapse after the teams had departed. In the summers, we did these trips back-to-back-to-back.

We worked with orphanages, local churches and a Mexican Baptist training institute. We sought out some of the poorest *colonias* (neighborhoods) in Matamoras. These *colonias* were infested with alcohol, hookers, rats, and drugs. We often slept in their shacks, in tents and in our vehicles as we wanted to remain as close to the people as we could throughout the week. The Lord allowed us entrance into the hearts of many people, some of whom became dear friends and believers in Christ.

However, the logistical burden of these trips was breaking us down. It was not uncommon to have a few dozen short-termers sleeping in our home at one time. On our record-setting night, we had 55 people sleeping in our house! All of our furniture was moved to the walls and we had them laid out on the floor like a morgue. There were people sleeping on couches, in chairs, and even stretched out on the trampoline in the backyard—those were the lucky ones. I actually stepped on a guy when I got out of my own bed in the middle of the night (several campers were asleep on our bedroom floor). These were wild days of reckless abandon. We said "yes" to everyone! "Always room for another dozen," I would frequently say. More than once, we had to call a professional plumber to regain use of our toilets after those weeks.

As hard as it was, it was an honor to carry Christ and the gospel into these dark, inner-city cesspools.

Mezquital

But I wasn't satisfied to stay only in the city. As desperately disadvantaged as Matamoras is, there are various brands of evangelical churches scattered around the city. I had a hankering to move farther south.

The most underprivileged and oppressed peoples are often those living in remote areas. Isolated communities are typically left out of development and educational opportunities, not to mention, being out of the reach of most missionaries. The sad result is that whole pockets of people are pushed to the side and left in hopeless conditions, essentially forgotten by the outside world. This is exactly the predicament I discovered on my initial visits to the Mezquital Islands.

The Port of Mezquital is strategically situated on the Gulf Coast, just eighty miles south of Matamoras and is the most prosperous village in the area. The Port of Mezquital, also known as "Fish Town," enjoys frequent visits from American short-term mission teams. There are several small Baptist and Pentecostal congregations in Fish Town, which serves as the literal "boat launch" to dozens of islands scattered across the Laguna Madre. These islands are home to thousands of people who make their meager living as fishermen.

The Island of Men—Ruby Island

My initial desire was to hire a boat and boatman to explore the various islands in the bay. On one of these trips, I was accompanied by my good friends, Tom Wallin and Steve Henry from Warsaw, Indiana. These guys are nearly as crazy as I am, and we were looking for lost "game."

The boatman had taken us to several islands throughout the day. Each one had small churches, which we were grateful for, so we moved along, still in search of gospel-less islands. As we were returning to Fish Town at the end of the day, I was disappointed that we had not located any truly "unreached" places. I saw an island that we had not visited off in the distance, and asked the boatman through a translator, "What about that island?" The boatman replied, "No, you don't want to go there. That's the *Island of Men*. It's an island of banished homosexual men!"

We all looked at each other bug-eyed and smiling. "That's exactly where we want to go! We have just the gospel for such a place as this!" We asked the boatman to take us there, but he emphatically refused.

Tom, Steve and I prayed about this island for a whole year. It became a primary goal to somehow get to the Island of Men on our next visit to Mezquital. Once again in Fish Town the following summer, we finally located a boatman name Felix, who agreed to drop us off on the island. As we traveled toward the Island of Men, several of us shared the gospel with Felix, through a translator. Felix replied, "I'm a Christian. I can't read or write, but what I've heard about Jesus, I believe!"

Felix didn't want to dock the boat, so we grabbed our gear and walked through knee-deep water to shore, and Felix sped off with the boat. The first thing we heard, once we got on shore, was the unexpected sound of children playing. A young man walked towards us. We explained our reason for coming, and he escorted us to the small one-room shack where he lived. *Beto* picked up a few of his belongings and told us that we could use his house. Just like that! He moved right out of his house for a group of unexpected, uninvited strangers.

Before long, an elderly woman and her husband came to see us. Carmen had beautiful white hair and a broad, full-faced, toothless smile. Through a translator, she excitedly told me that her parents had told her about Christ when she was a child. She prayed for many years that someone would bring the gospel to her island. Then she shocked me by saying, "I knew you were coming today!" I asked her what she meant.

She replied, "Jesus told me you were coming today! No one has visited our island in 27 years…We feel like we have been abandoned by God… All we want is for someone to teach us the Word of God."

We were all wiping our tears. I told Carmen through a translator that

David with Carmen, Island of Men (Ruby Island), Mezquital, Mexico (2003)

I wanted to kiss her. She smiled and said, "Kiss me!"

I kissed the top of her head and told her, "I see Jesus in your face." She quickly responded, "He lives in my heart and comes out of my face!" What a remarkable woman! Both she and her husband were believers in Christ and are now with the Lord.

As for the Island of Men, it was not an island of homosexuals. That was a complete fabrication of the enemy of souls, as a ploy to keep the island far away from the gospel. Tom Wallin and a few others have continued their ministry there sporadically over the years and several villagers on the island have come to faith and been baptized in the Laguna Madre.

The stories of gospel advance on the Island of Men, Media Luna, Emiliano Zapata, and Centenario would fill more than one book. Our friends, Steve and Robin Henry, relocated several years ago to La Poza and have a good foothold for the gospel there as well.

Ministry and Staff Expansion

More than 3,000 people joined us on short-term ministry trips over a period of ten years. These years of vigorous short-term mis-

sion activity and travel among stateside churches was beginning
to bring about a mobilization of on-ground reinforcement that
Tommi and I desperately needed.

A major breakthrough came with a phone call from Steve Henry
in 2003 telling me that he and Robin were seriously praying about
joining us full-time in South Texas. This was great news to us. Steve
and Robin were good friends and gifted in ways that significantly
complimented Tommi and me. Steve had been the Missions Pastor
at Christ's Covenant Church, in Warsaw, Indiana, which was one
of our long-time supporting churches. Steve and Robin arrived
in the summer of 2004.

Almost immediately, *To Every Tribe* organized a board of directors
and gained its 501 (C-3) non-profit tax-status.

The Center For Pioneer Church Planting (CPCP)

Because there are so many ripe regions and so few workers,
I dreamed for more than fifteen years about establishing a missionary training center. However, until Steve and Robin joined
us, it was never within our reach. But with Steve and Robin's
assistance, the encouragement of our newly formed board, and
the addition of my good friend David Harrell, from Dayspring
Fellowship in Austin, as our first Executive Director, things
began to happen quickly.

Our first board meeting was hosted by another long-time supporting congregation, Reformed Baptist Church, in Lewisburg,
PA. Reformed Baptist was hosting a Missions Conference during that same weekend. In one of my messages, I mentioned our
rapid growth and the need for additional stateside staff. My good
friend Rod Conner had served as pastor of Reformed Baptist
for twenty-three years. He had recently resigned but was still a
member there. After hearing my plea for more staff, he invited

me to an evening meal. It didn't take Rod and Linda long to decide to join forces with us, and they quickly raised their support to come on as full-time staff. Since then, Rod has become our Vice-President.

The additions of Steve and Robin Henry, David Harrell and Rod Conner enabled us to seriously brainstorm about the beginning of a missionary training program. The Center For Pioneer Church Planting (CPCP) became a reality with a first class of five full-time students on January 9, 2006. The CPCP was the culmination of many years of my own preparation through on-the-job training, much prayer and planning, and a gifted group of men who could help me do it. From the beginning, our goal was to invest 40 percent of the training time in the mentoring of our trainees through on-the-job training exploits in PNG and Mexico.

One of the pressing needs of our time is for the right kind of missionary training. We live in a day of heightened missions awareness; tens of thousands of young people go all over the world on all kinds of mission trips. That could be a good thing. However, there is a danger in what Ralph Winter called, "the amateurization of missions," meaning, there is a serious lack of adequate missions preparedness for those who desire to pursue longer-term missionary ministry. And one of the sad results of insufficient preparation is an incredibly high missionary failure rate.

To Every Tribe is primarily a cross-cultural, pioneer church planting ministry. Everything we do is directly related to establishing worshipping communities of new Jesus followers in places where there is presently no evangelical witness for the gospel. However, to facilitate responsible church planting in a bigger way, faster and in more locations simultaneously, it is imperative that we reproduce ourselves as quickly as possible in young people who will then charge into the nations with the gospel well beyond our own lifetimes. They will then, Lord enabling, reproduce themselves into third, fourth and fifth generations of church planters. This is the passion that compelled us to birth the CPCP.

David Sitton and John Piper, Purpose-Driven
Death Mission Conference (2008)

Chapter 17
The Bethlehem Tithe

WE WERE BUSY WITH OUR church planting ministry in Papua New Guinea in 1989 when I first heard the name of John Piper. Jackson Boyett, pastor of our home church, Dayspring Fellowship, in Austin, Texas, brought a set of cassette tapes when he and his wife Barbara visited us in New Guinea. Jackson and I listened carefully as John explained the concept of Christian hedonism as described in his book, *Desiring God*.

John's bald-faced passion for Jesus, coupled with his gutsy, Holy Spirit-empowered preaching, forcibly connected with my soul. John's ministry at Bethlehem Baptist in Minneapolis, was a world away from us in Papua New Guinea, yet as the years rolled along someone would occasionally send us a new Piper book. We became cheerleaders from across the sea as John articulated, in anointed ways through print and preaching, God's heart for all nations to know and worship the King.

It would be nineteen years before I would personally meet pastor John. A good friend, Hutz Hertzberg, Executive Pastor to Dr. Erwin Lutzer at the Moody Church in Chicago, knew Dr. Piper. Hutz had sent my book, *To Every Tribe With Jesus*, along with one of my preaching CDs and a personal note to John. In July 2005, quite unexpectedly, Dr. Piper called and asked if I would be the mission speaker at the upcoming Bethlehem Pastors Conference in Minneapolis in

February 2006. I immediately accepted and called Jackson Boyett to tell him, and ask him to come to the conference with me.

A few months later, because I was visiting several churches in Minnesota, I emailed Dr. Piper and asked if he would meet me for lunch since we had never met. I arrived at his home on a blustery, cold November day. The wind was blowing 25 miles an hour, and I was dressed in a lightweight business suit because I was preaching later that day in St. Paul. John invited me into his home and introduced me to his wife Noël and his daughter Talitha. We sat and talked for a bit in his living room.

After lunch at a nearby restaurant, we returned to his home. I had become chilled in the bitter cold and was noticeably uncomfortable as we were saying goodbye in his living room. John suddenly said, "You can't leave in this cold weather dressed in a Texas suit!" He opened a closet and retrieved a full-length trench coat that hit me below the knees.

Noël walked by and added, "He can't go out with just a coat; he needs a scarf also!" She pulled one off of a hanger in the closet and wrapped it around my neck. That was my introduction to the graciousness of John and Noël Piper.

Prayer and Fasting

As I prepared to speak at the Bethlehem Pastors Conference, my journal entry for January 11, 2006 says:

> I'm really beginning to feel the pressure of my message for the conference. I'm having a difficult time getting my thoughts together for it. I've been told that the conference is completely sold out which means there will be 1,400 pastors there. Lord, give me a message and help me to deliver it.

I taught today in our Center for Pioneer Church Planting on prayer and fasting. I challenged our students to a four-week fast with two purposes in mind. One is for any personal issue that they may have in their own lives. Secondly, we will pray and fast for the upcoming Bethlehem Pastors Conference, that the Lord will compel 140 pastors to resign their present positions in order to take the gospel to the nations. I've been impressed and praying for some time that the Lord will give me a "tithe" of those pastors for unreached peoples.

The week before the conference began with a series of specific spiritual attacks. First a large, painful boil appeared on my neck. Then, I contracted pink eye in both eyes which lasted for several days, with high fever and headaches almost every day and a bad cough. Needless to say, it was all a distraction whenever I tried to concentrate and study for the message.

Our *To Every Tribe* staff and CPCP students continued to pray daily and fast weekly for the specific number of 140 pastors to be dislodged and immediately re-deployed to unreached places. I was convinced the Lord was about to do something significant.

John had asked me to speak on the subject of suffering, hardship, persecution and martyrdom in mission. The actual title to the message became *Missionary Martyrs: Fools for Jesus—For the Nations*.

I left for Minneapolis a few hours earlier than Tommi and my children, Joshua, Barbara and Jimmy because the conference planners had arranged a private, pre-conference catered meal for the speakers.. By the time I arrived, my persistent cough had intensified. I was physically weak and increasingly nervous about my part of the conference, but the meal was a good time to meet the other speakers and try to settle myself down.

After the meal, I asked to see the conference center. Walking into the massive room, I felt as though I had been sucker-punched! I shuddered at the sight of 1,400 empty chairs. It seriously scared me, and I hurried up to my hotel room. I began to doubt that I had the right message for the occasion and felt a webbed net of fear beginning to wrap itself around me.

People who loved me were genuinely excited about this great opportunity for me to speak to a large group of influential pastors and mission leaders. But they were all hustling around, busy with conference details, while I was alone in my room in a desperate panic.

As the conference progressed, I was convinced that I could not preach. I felt trapped. The afternoon before I was to speak the following morning, I was in seclusion in my hotel room. My entire body quivered with fear of what was about to happen. This was not the normal anxiety that often comes with public speaking. It was purebred debilitating distress! My misery was intensifying and my cough was uncontrollable whenever I tried to talk.

The night before I was to speak, Tommi and I, along with the other speakers, were invited to John and Noël's home for dinner. I really didn't want to be there because I was physically sick, edgy, and embarrassed by my conversation-killing cough. As the dinner was coming to an end and the dishes were removed from the table, John suddenly stopped talking to Ajith Fernando and Michael Campbell. He looked me straight in the eyes, pointed at me and said, "David, I'm praying that God will release 150 pastors for the nations tomorrow morning through your ministry!" John knew nothing about our praying and fasting for 140 and didn't realize that he had just upped the ante by ten!

I was shocked at his statement and asked, "John, why did you say 150?" He raised both hands, palms up and fingers spread wide, flashed a grin and said, "I don't know why I said 150. Receive it as a gift from God!" What an incredibly, prophetic moment!

John gathered the speakers in his living room to pray. I pulled a small flask of anointing oil out of my pocket and handed it to John. These brothers anointed me with oil and prayed for me, as James 5:13-16 instructs us to do in situations where we are in trouble or need healing and help from the Holy Spirit. One thing John prayed has stayed with me. He said, "Please, Lord, give David an hour and a half without coughing to deliver your message!"

I sat out Ajith's last message that evening, holed up in my hotel room trying to get myself together. A physical and emotional mess, I was unable even to look at my message notes. Unknown to me, Tommi went to find Jackson and told him, "David needs you!"

Jackson gathered up my friends Steve Henry and Rod Conner and they marched into my room like soldiers on a mission! Jackson asked me to join them in his room. I walked wobbly-kneed down the hall and flopped into a chair, physically, mentally and spiritually done, totally at the end of myself, and resigned to a coming fiasco the following morning.

Without speaking, I pulled the oil container out of my pocket again and gave it to Jackson. He smiled, hugged me, knelt on the floor and began putting oil on me and praying. Actually, it wasn't even praying—it was more like a fistfight with the devil! I could feel Jackson prying the enemy off of me, one demon after another, some of them even by name, and all of them in Jesus' name. He rebuked the devourer and simply committed me to the grace of God, that I would be mightily used for God's glory and for the advance of the gospel. Steve Henry told me later that he had never witnessed such powerful ministry before and that I looked physically different afterwards, as though I had been visibly delivered from something.

Very little was said by anyone afterwards. Jackson told me to go to bed. I walked slowly back to my room. Something had changed in me that I was unable to identify just then. I was so exhausted I fell asleep almost immediately. I awoke at 4:11 AM (the bright red hotel room clock said so). There was an implausible calmness in my spirit and a sense of purpose and confidence that I did, in fact, have the message that God wanted to deliver. I stayed in bed for an hour and a half, just resting in the Spirit of God. I repeated over and over in my mind, "Thank you for this peace. I don't understand how this is possible, but thank you, Lord, for settling my heart."

After showering, I went to the prayer room early. I was the only one there for a while, sitting quietly and calmly. However, I was still coughing quite a lot even there. Eventually, Piper and a few others arrived and prayed with me again.

Then it was time to get wired with the microphone as the service began. The singing was incredible in every service, but it seemed exceptional that morning, as more than 1,400 men worshipped with upbeat praise to the God of all nations.

A Time to Speak

Jackson had commandeered the seat closest to the lectern. Dr. Piper introduced me very graciously, though I don't remember anything he said. Then, our *To Every Tribe* DVD was shown. When it was almost over, I leaned over to Tommi, who I knew was scared silly for me. "Tommi, it's ok. I feel great. I'm hardly nervous at all." I timed my walk to the pulpit so I would get there as the DVD ended. A spotlight hit me full in the face as I opened my notes and Bible.

All I can say—trite but true—is that the Spirit of God "fell" forcefully on me! I have never experienced such a combination of the Holy Spirit, clarity of thought and control, mixed with holy boldness, as I did in that moment. It was an awesome outpouring of grace upon me and the entire room. Even as I spoke, I became aware of pockets of men weeping around the room.

This was a heavy duty, take up your cross, go to the nations and die as a martyr kind of message. But the impact of it came from the immediately powerful way the Holy Spirit applied it to the hearts of men and women.

At one point, I made a humorous comment and many of the men laughed. However, one man jumped up and started yelling and rebuking the crowd. I thought he was rebuking me at first because I couldn't understand everything he was shouting. But I did hear him yell, "Gentlemen! That's not funny! This is serious stuff!" Then he ran to the back of the conference room, stopped, looked back at me and yelled again, "Thank you David!" And he stormed out of the room and down the hall.

I looked down at Piper who was sitting on the front row. He just gave me his palms up, fingers outstretched gesture, grinning at me.

What the enemy intended to be a distraction, actually achieved the opposite. There was even more seriousness, soberness and more weeping in various places around the room as I continued. I spoke for more than an hour and a half. A couple of times I looked at my watch, and men yelled out, "Forget the time. Keep going!"

I closed the message with a challenge, explaining how the Lord had impressed me to ask Him for a tithe of them for the nations. "How are you going to invest your lives, right now, for Christ, for the gospel and for the nations? I'm calling upon a tithe of you men to resign your pastorates, get the necessary training and quickly redeploy to unreached regions." I read Psalm 96 and walked off of the stage.

I don't remember how the service ended. But I was immediately surrounded by dozens of pastors, many of them crying and pressing through the crowd to speak to me. People were hugging me and whispering in my ear, "I'm part of the tithe! I'm one of the 140!"

Someone requested a picture of John and me, and we were squeezed together. John put his arm around my shoulder and whispered into my ear, "In the years to come, people will be talking about Sitton's tithe for the nations and what God did on February 1, 2006!"

It was so humbling he would say that to me. Time didn't permit for me to speak privately again with John, during the conference. However, we did have a speakers' Q & A that I barely remember, except that I left in the middle of it. I was sitting on the far-left end of the Q & A table with Ajith Fernando sitting to my right. I hadn't been to the bathroom for many hours and was about to explode. I leaned over and told Ajith where I had to go. He just looked at me and grinned. As I exited, literally stage left, and headed for the bathroom, I heard Piper say, "I'll let David answer that...where did David go?"

Later, at our ministry table for three and a half hours, I had been mobbed by dozens of pastors. I talked to everyone who was willing to wait. Many of them wanted to tell me that they were a part of the tithe. That evening I realized that in those ten hours since being in the prayer room, I had only coughed twice!

Remembrance and Praise to God

No one knows better than me what an outpouring of grace and Holy Spirit power had been dumped on me that morning!

I often reflect upon the beginning of the conference when I walked into the empty conference room and a spirit of fear attached itself to me. I became completely terrorized and immobilized by it. There was sin in me that I didn't even realize until the enemy made it clear. It was the sin of wanting to be significant, wanting to say something important and profound. There was in my heart, with the enemy's prompting, thoughts like, "This is your chance for recognition!"

There were also thoughts of wanting to please John Piper, which in itself was not altogether bad. Naturally, I wanted him to be pleased with the ministry of the Word through me. He took a risk—bigger than he realized—in asking me to speak, and I didn't want him to regret his choice.

All that rubbish coupled with the normal apprehension of a large venue made me spiritually vulnerable. The enemy pounced on me in an attempt to destroy the moment. But, once again, he was rebuked by our great God. Through Jackson Boyett's prayer and those of so many of my friends, the Lord used me incredibly right at the moment of my complete inadequacy. The Lord ruled over all of my weakness, fears, and sinful passions, and I believe a great blow was struck for the Kingdom of God on that Wednesday morning, February 1, 2006.

In the week after the conference before I left on a trip to PNG, nearly fifty pastors contacted me through emails, letters and phone calls. The tithe continues to roll in today, years later, as pastors who were there that morning come to work with us as staff. The Center For Pioneer Church Planting continues to expand with single people and young families who were either directly or indirectly through their pastors, challenged to "sell out and go" as martyr missionaries to all peoples.[86]

Jackson Boyett told me later he had heard me preach dozens of times, but never with such power and anointing as that morning. I have asked the Lord several times why he doesn't use me more frequently that way. It seems the answer, ironically, is because I am

---

86   Ron and Margie Sanford, Stephanie Dupraw, A.J. and Ruth Gibson, Bob and Mary Warman and Steve and Terri Best have all become indispensable additions to our ministry, either directly or indirectly as a result of the Bethlehem tithe.

not usually *weak enough* to be used so powerfully. Isn't it true that often our ministries are less Holy Spirit-empowered than they could be, simply because we come with so much of our own (perceived) competence and ministry capability? I pray (though hesitantly, I admit) that God will make me *weak enough* to use me more often in the gospel, "not with wise and persuasive words, but with a demonstration of the Spirit's power."[87]

David and Tommi Sitton

---

87   I Corinthians 2:4

Chapter 18
Airmailed to Jesus

In Memory of Makayla Joy Sitton
December 6, 2002 – November 26, 2009

MANY WHO READ THIS BOOK, which includes accounts of violence done to Christians in a primitive society, might shake their heads and even thank God that they don't live in a place such as Papua New Guinea. But glancing at any newspaper reminds us we live in a world full of evil. While my family was protected during our times in PNG, unimaginable violence reached into our extended family in the "safety" of the U.S. This is the story of my niece Makayla, to whom this book is dedicated, a little girl who loved Jesus fully in her short life.

On Thanksgiving night, 2009, at the home of my brother Jim and his wife Muriel, in Jupiter, Florida, an extended family member, calmly left the home, walked to his car and returned with two guns. He then re-entered the kitchen scattering shots in all directions. Within seconds, he sprayed more than fifteen shots throughout four rooms.

When it was over, the gunman had killed five people: his own two twin sisters (one of them pregnant), his aunt (Muriel's mother), and Jim and Muriel's only daughter, six-year-old Makayla, who had just been tucked into bed shortly before the shooting started.

: : : : : :

Earlier that afternoon, the Sitton home had been a peaceful scene of praise and gratitude to God and Makayla had been completely in the moment. She loved family celebrations and spent the day helping her mom, Muriel, in preparation for the Thanksgiving gathering.

Following the dinner, the family had gathered in the living room around the piano for a special time of praise and thanksgiving. Makayla had thoughtfully planned out a program and rehearsed it earlier in the day with her mom. She played several songs on the piano, danced to hymns, sang "Man of Sorrows," and recited Psalm 100 from memory. Others joined in the singing as well—it was a joyous time of giving thanks to God. At one point, Makayla asked her dad if she could say something that was on her heart to the family.

Makayla encouraged her family that Thanksgiving is not just a time of eating lots of good food and being merry. But rather, faith in Jesus is something that should be communicated. If "thanks" isn't spoken, then it's not really "thanks-giving" but only "thanks-feeling." She went on to say, "So that is what we are doing here tonight, we're giving thanks to God." It was a beautifully mature expression of what a passion for Jesus will produce in a person's life. Makayla was a genuinely grateful and thoughtful child.

The killer, I am told, sat through the program, quiet and away from the family in a corner, all the while watching Makayla's straightforward love and witness for Jesus.

Afterwards it was bedtime for Makayla. Jim and Muriel tucked her in, not realizing that it would be for the last time.

The shooting started shortly thereafter. Jim quickly tried to direct stunned family members to safety, and was able to escape being shot himself by slipping through the sliding glass door onto the back porch. His wife Muriel was able to run for cover in the laundry room and eventually escaped outside and found Jim. At that point she screamed, "Get Makayla, get Makayla!" They both ran around to the front of the house where Makayla's bedroom was, to get their daughter out. Muriel tried to open the front door but it was locked.

Muriel watched the shadow of the gunman (her cousin) helplessly through a window as he walked down the hallway toward Makayla's bedroom. Jim was desperately trying to break through the storm window of Makayla's bedroom when he saw the light flashes from the gun and heard the quick succession of several gun shots.

Makayla's short life was suddenly and brutally crushed.

The gunman slaughtered Makayla with several point-blank gunshots to her head and chest. Looking back on the horror of that night, and given the benefit of time, I can now only imagine that the killer must have hated what Makayla represented. He must have hated the light. It seems the spiritual darkness within him couldn't endure the light and life of the gospel, and he tried to extinguish it with a vengeance.

Jim and Muriel were left broken and devastated. But in the midst of our family's great sorrow and pain, we as Christians clung to the truth, that he was able to kill her body, but he couldn't ultimately hurt her.[88] His evil intentions immediately put her in the arms of Jesus forever.[89] Makayla was safely airmailed to Jesus.

Solomon wrote, "The day of death is better than the day of birth" (Ecclesiastes 7:1). A stunning truth for believers in Jesus: our *death date* is far more significant than our *birth date*. Birth dates signal the inauguration of trouble and hardship that will hound us every day that we live. However, the moment of death, for believers, signals the eternal end to the afflictions of what it is to be a human being.

---

88 This is what Jesus meant when he said "And they will put some of you to death...but not a hair of your head will perish." Luke 21:16-18. Enemies of the gospel can kill our bodies but they can't ultimately hurt us.

89 Psalm 116:15; 2 Corinthians 5:8

"Write this: Blessed are the dead who die in the Lord from now on." "Blessed indeed," says the Spirit, "that they may rest from their labors, for their deeds follow them!"[90]

Whatever the exact time of death was for Makayla, that was the moment she first looked fully into the face of Christ.

> *Death doesn't get the last word*
> *In the end, it will not speak*
> *Death is our last enemy*
> *Jesus will turn its other cheek*
> *Into the Lake of Fire*[91]

Justice Delayed

Jim and Muriel were both in the television industry, and the news media covered the crime and search for the killer extensively. Jim is an Emmy-winning special projects photographer, editor and video journalist with the NBC affiliate in West Palm Beach, Florida. Muriel, a former Emmy-winning writer and producer herself, had left the news business and devoted her time to children's ministry and homeschooling Makayla.

The graveside and memorial service for Makayla was held under heavy police and FBI protection because they feared that her killer would come back and try to kill more of the family. However, he had escaped from the area and the trail went cold. The wife of John Walsh's *America's Most Wanted* (*AMW*) heard the news report and urged John to help our family. It became one of the program's priority cases. One night, more than a month after the murders, *AMW* was scheduled to highlight the case again for their Saturday night show. Earlier in the day the network played a promo showing a picture of the murderer—Paul Merhige. The owners of a small hotel

90   Revelation 14:13
91   Poem by David Sitton, based upon 1 Corinthians 15:26 and Revelation 20:4

in the Florida Keys saw his picture and realized he was holed up in one of their rooms. They called the *AMW* hotline and following the confirmation of his license plate, U.S. Marshals, local police, and FBI agents surrounded the hotel. When they busted through the door, they captured him. The television was turned to *AMW*. He had been watching himself on TV.

At the time of this writing, Merhige is in jail awaiting trial. It has been nearly two years since the murders. The prosecution plans to seek the death penalty, and our family hopes that justice delayed will not be justice denied.[92]

Makayla Joy Sitton (May, 2009 – Six months before the murders)

---

92 Further information about Makayla may be accessed at: *http://makayla-joysitton.com.*

Chapter 19
Jesus Is Worth It!

"Preach the gospel, die and be forgotten."
—COUNT NIKOLAS ZINZENDORF
Founder of the Moravians

THE MONTH BEFORE MAKAYLA WAS murdered, *To Every Tribe* hosted, along with the Kinsey Drive Baptist Church, our annual mission conference in Dalton, Georgia. The theme of the conference was *The Privilege of Suffering: Jesus is Worth It!* I am convinced this is a message the comfortable, at-ease American church needs to hear. However, I never speak of missionary suffering and persecution without great trepidation. My so-called *sufferings* experienced on long bush-whacking hikes through the jungles: enduring malarial and dengue fevers, the loneliness of long separations from family and friends, and being physically slapped around a little because of Jesus, though significant to me, are infinitesimally small in comparison to the sufferings of so many. Certainly these puny adversities cannot be compared to the sufferings of Christ or the horrific injustices that are inflicted upon tens of thousands of believers every year—just because they believe in Jesus. Furthermore, my trials are not even to be mentioned in a discussion of the unspeakable desolation of spirit I have witnessed in Jim and Muriel following the brutal slaughter of Makayla.

But this I know: *Jesus is worth it!* There is no point in which Jesus and the gospel are no longer worth the sacrifice. Moreover, suffering such as this, actually catapults the gospel even more speedily into new regions. This is one of the great mysteries of how God has divinely chosen to propel and permeate His name throughout the earth. Makayla advanced the gospel far more widely in death than she ever could have in life. Within hours, her testimony of faith went around the world! Makayla has joined a select group that has been privileged to "not only believe on him, but also to suffer for him"[93] through particularly tough circumstances, but always for the purpose of glorifying God.

As I observe Jim and Muriel go on with their lives, it is only because of Jesus that they can do so. They remind me of another of my heroes, the Scottish missionary John Paton who buried one wife and five children in the New Hebrides Islands. How could he do that? Why did he not just quit and go home after the death of his first or fourth child? Because Jesus and the gospel are worth it; there is no other plausible reply.

In the months after Makayla was killed, I spent a lot of time pondering the meaning of her life, the way she died and the chaos and suffering our entire family was immediately buried beneath. I do not have definitive answers to every question. But here is where I find rest: "Our citizenship is in heaven. And we eagerly await a Savior from there, the Lord Jesus Christ, who, *by the power that enables Him to bring everything under His control*, will transform our lowly bodies so that they will be like His glorious body."[94]

Oftentimes, the only thing one can do is to suffer within the hands of the One who is able to bring everything under control. But it's more than that. God doesn't just "manage the damage," He definitively promises "to work everything for the good of those who love Him, who have been called according to His purpose."[95]

One result of our tragedy is that we all hold much more loosely to this life which Scripture calls a "mist that appears for a little while

---

93   Philippians 1:29
94   Philippians 3:20-21
95   Romans 8:28

and then vanishes."[96] Makayla reminded us that we are only passers-by in this world, and I think we all live with a looser grip on it.

Violent Faith and Forgiving Our Enemies

I saw a quote recently: "If there is one maverick molecule, then God isn't sovereign. If God isn't sovereign, then God isn't God."[97] We are not at the ultimate mercy of a maverick molecule or a malevolent madman. At the same time, we can't choose our sufferings or protect our children with infallible safety by wrapping them in bubble wrap. But we can find rest and relief in a sovereign God who oversees the fall of every sparrow from the sky.

God has promised deliverance to believers in Christ. But there are two ways in which deliverance may come. We may be delivered *from* death so that we can live to further advance the gospel with our mouths.[98] Or, we may be delivered *through* death, as countless martyrs through the centuries have been, instantly ushered into the presence of Christ, but still advancing the gospel with our blood. We either win by living, and the world gets more of Jesus from us. Or we win really big by dying, and we get more of Jesus in His presence![99] The one thing we cannot do is "lose our lives" for the gospel. That is impossible. We can only "gain our lives" if "we lose them" and if we die physically, we gain them even quicker.[100]

Violent faith such as this is dangerous to the kingdom of darkness. When we no longer live in fear of death, we are liberated to glorify God in a more powerful way. We walk into the world wielding the faith of weak and foolish lambs against voracious and clever lions. But this is precisely God's strategy for victory; God always conquers through weakness, death, and resurrection. It is by God's

---

96   James 4:14
97   R.C. Sproul
98   2 Corinthians 1:8-11
99   Philippians 1:20-21
100 Matthew 10:39; Luke 9:24

power, through the blood of the Lamb and through the blood of His lambs[101] that the Kingdom advances throughout the world.[102]

There is, however, another weapon of warfare with which we must fight during our pilgrimage upon this evil earth. We forgive our enemies! This is a hard word that only the recklessly abandoned can hear and embrace. At no other time are we more like God than when we forgive our enemies.

"I tell you: Love your enemies and pray for those who persecute you, that you may be *sons of your Father in heaven*."[103] Jesus says that forgiving enemies who persecute us is a characteristic that sets us apart from "pagans."

At *To Every Tribe*, we often talk about "loving the hate out of people." The Apostle Paul says it this way, "Bless those that persecute you; bless and do not curse… Do not be overcome by evil, but overcome evil with good."[104] This is not human! It is completely otherworldly, but it's a cross-cultural concept that we must learn as we become citizens of heaven. I'm not completely there yet. But I must take this to heart if I want to be a "son of my Father in heaven."

A Personal Interjection

As I press along into my middle 50's I'm young enough, by God's grace, to still have some years left in me. I still have some licks to land for the gospel! But I'm old enough to see the finish line quickly approaching. I find myself constantly reevaluating my life and ministry. How can I best invest the remainder of my days, most productively, in getting the message of the cross established among the least-reached peoples of the world?

A Purpose-Driven Death

To Every Tribe hosted a mission conference in Austin, Texas in 2008 with the theme: The Purpose-Driven *Death*. We received a good amount of pushback because of this radical emphasis. Why all the controversy?

---

101 Revelation 12:11
102 Acts 5:40-42; Acts 6:6; Acts 8:1-4; Philippians 1:12-14
103 Matthew 5:43-48; Matthew 6:12-15
104 Romans 12:14, 21

Why do American believers assume that they are somehow exempt from ultimate "sacrifices" for the sake of Christ and the gospel? Why are there so few modern-day martyrs from the Western world?

"If God is for us, who can be against us? He who did not spare his own Son, but gave him up for us all, how will he not also with him graciously give us all things."[105] What is included in "all things"? Part of our privilege was foreseen by the Psalmist and reiterated here by the Apostle Paul, "For your sake we face death all day long; we are considered as sheep to be slaughtered."[106]

If you have never considered the possibility that *God loves you and may have a wonderful plan for your death*, perhaps you should. He had a wonderful plan for the death of His Son. He had a wonderful plan for the Ecuador Five who were slaughtered in the jungle of Ecuador—a plan that resulted in the Waodani tribe responding to the gospel en masse and launching two generations of tens of thousands of new missionaries over the last fifty years to some of the toughest unreached regions in the world.

Why is the *The Purpose-Driven Life* a runaway bestseller, but the concept of a strategically purposed laying down of life and limb for Jesus among militant Muslims, for example, considered risky and even foolhardy?

It is my conviction as a mission leader, rather than encouraging this generation of young believers to pad their IRA retirement accounts, we should be pointing them towards packing their own coffins with a few belongings as they set sail for the strongholds of Satan in the 10 / 40 Window[107] countries.

That's what Fijian believers did in the early 1840's.[108] As the gospel made its way into Fiji for the first time, a large number of

---

105 Romans 8:31-32
106 Psalm 44:22; Romans 8:36
107 The 10/40 Window is the geographic area between the latitudes 10 and 40 degrees north of the equator and between the Atlantic and Pacific Oceans.
108 The story of these South Pacific Island missionaries can be read in the excellent book, The Deep-Sea Canoe, by Alan R. Tippett (Christian Books Melanesia Inc., P.O. Box 488, Wewak, E.S.P. Papua New Guinea, 1994).

Polynesians were radically converted to Christ. The Lord began to give them a heart for mission, and they decided they wanted to take the gospel to New Guinea because they had heard of the cannibals there. These Fijians had been cannibals themselves just a few years previously. They had heard the gruesome stories about the wild, cannibalizing, headhunting tribes of New Guinea. They knew that many of their number would probably be killed and eaten. Do you know what they did? They each built their own coffins, packed their belongings into them, and sailed thousands of miles across the South Pacific on their deep-sea canoes, landing on the South Coast of New Guinea in 1871.

One Fijian evangelist expressed the attitude of these Polynesian missionaries as they prepared to set sail. He wrote in his journal, "We died before we left!" This brother and many of those with him were quickly killed and eaten by those they tried to tell about Christ. Many Fijian believers became missionary martyrs. One story tells how a Fijian evangelist was killed and cannibalized. When news reached Fiji about the slaughter of the missionaries, one man, whose own brother had been cannibalized, stood up in the meeting and said, "Now I must go and take my brother's place on the front line!" He packed his coffin and immediately left for New Guinea as a missionary replacement for his brother.

These are the kinds of missionaries the church needs, and I'm on the lookout for them. I'm on a crusade to recruit *Navy Seals* missionaries! I want the *First Responders* for the cause of Christ, those who are willing to charge into impossible near-suicide situations, simply because Jesus and the gospel are worth the risk! I'm searching for the *recklessly abandoned*, martyr missionaries who are willing to go and die, and for those God-glorifying financial martyrs who will recklessly die to their financial interests in order to get these missionaries quickly deployed to the ends of the earth.

Epilogue

I HAD THE UNEXPECTED PLEASURE in April, 2011 to meet with a few dozen Kukakuka believers who now live in the Tent City section of Lae, the coastal city in Papua New Guinea where my journey in mission first began in 1977. One of the leading men, Woponoko, eagerly arranged a special gathering with me and a handful of these Menyamya believers. Woponoko lives with his wife in a run-down, dirt-floor shack. The campfire is situated in a corner of the hut because more than half the roof has caved in. Half of the hut is literally "under the stars" each evening. Underneath this makeshift house, the Menyamyas placed a carpet of palm leaves for me to sit on, and they provided a modest meal for me. I sat and reminisced with the older believers. There were hugs, lots of laughter and tears of happiness at being together again.

I showed them some old pictures from the late 70's, and we determined that Woponoko is the son and nephew of two of the very first tribal chiefs who were converted. In typically animated Menyamya manner, Woponoko shouted to me, "You started out as a missionary with us and you must die (end) with us as a missionary!"

I had not seen the Menyamya believers for nearly thirty years, but they are still going strong for Jesus! The gospel, often through hardship, is widely advancing. God had said to me "go" many years before, and I had followed His voice. Had I clung to my surfboard and the comfortable, easy self-focused life I loved so much, I would have missed an exciting adventure far beyond anything I could have dreamed or imagined for myself.

God rescued this once lost surfer boy, changed me into a God-worshipper—a radical Jesus follower. He has allowed me to be His co-worker in the gospel to the nations. The privilege of my life is that I wear the name "Christian" and that the Lord compelled my heart to go into the difficult regions of Menyamya among the Kukakukas, a formerly cannibalistic people, to Rakamunda where they had never seen a white man or heard the name of Christ, and to the Chambri who had been a headhunting tribe a generation ago and were exceedingly hostile when they first heard the gospel.

The thrill of my life now is that my children in mission are radically and joyfully going into the dangerous regions of Papua New Guinea and Mexico while others are scheming ways to make inroads for Christ and the gospel among still unreached, often resistant, sometimes violent Muslim peoples.

In all of these places and many more—hundreds more in the future, I pray—the Lord has made it the joy of my life to be one of his gospel ambassadors, a fool for Jesus for unreached nations and a pioneer church planting missionary, commissioned by God to "go and get some of them for Jesus!"

End Notes

INTRODUCTION: FOOTNOTE #7. HERE IS the complete letter that Ed McCully sent to Jim Elliot:

Since taking this job things have happened. I've been spending my free time studying the Word. Each night the Lord seemed to get hold of me a little more. Night before last, I was reading in Nehemiah. I finished the book and read it through again. Here was a man who left everything as far as position was concerned to go do a job nobody else could handle. And because he went, the whole remnant back in Jerusalem got right with the Lord. Obstacles and hindrances fell away and a great work was done.

Jim, I couldn't get away from it. The Lord was dealing with me. On the way home yesterday morning, I took a long walk and came to a decision which I know is of the Lord. In all honesty before the Lord, I say that no one or nothing beyond himself and the Word has any bearing upon what I have decided to do. *I have one desire now – to live a life of reckless abandon for the Lord, putting all my energy into it. Maybe he'll send me some place where the name of Jesus Christ is unknown.* Jim, I'm taking the Lord at his Word, and I trust him to prove his Word. It's kind of like putting all your eggs in one basket, but we've already put our trust in him for salvation, so why not do it as far as our life is concerned? If there is nothing to this business of eternal life, we might as well lose everything in one crack and throw our present life away without life hereafter.

But if there is something to it, then everything else the Lord says must hold true likewise. Pray for me, Jim.

Man, to think the Lord got hold of me just one day before I was to register for school! I've got money put away and was all set to go. Today was registration, so I went over to school to let them know why I wouldn't be back. I really prayed like the Apostle asked the Ephesians to pray, that I might "open my mouth boldly." I talked to all the fellows that I knew well. Then I went in to see a professor I thought a lot about. I told him what I planned to do, and before I left he had tears in his eyes. I went to see another professor and talked to him. All I got was a cold farewell and a good luck wish.

Well, that's it. Two days ago I was a law student. Today, I'm an untitled nobody. Thanks, Jim, for the intercession on my behalf. Don't let up. And brother, I'm really praying for you too as you're making preparation to leave. I only wish I were going with you.

—ED McCULLY

Endorsements Continued

OUR WORLD IS CHANGING SO dramatically that missions struggle to keep pace. *Pioneering, casting a vision, meeting needs, transforming lives*—even *risk-taking*—all are still very much parts of the vocabulary of Christian missions today. But they are almost invariably related to mission theology and theory, not so often to missionary practice. In this respect, David Sitton and his book *Reckless Abandon* will be seen by some as hopelessly out of date. But they are happily up to date in another and much more important respect. They are "right on" simply because the world is not changing for the better; people are still sinners and need saving; the gospel is still the power of God unto salvation; and biblical mission is still focused on proclaiming the gospel to the unreached and planting churches throughout the world. So read this book, let its message permeate your mind and heart, and then recommend it to your friends. You and they will find it to be reminiscent of the account of Adoniram Judson and the outgrowth of a Haystack Prayer Meeting at Williams College in the early 19th century; of C. T. Studd and the exploits of the Cambridge Seven at the end of the 19th; and of the unforgettable story of Jim Elliot and the Auca Martyrs in the middle of the 20th.

—DAVID J. HESSELGRAVE, PH.D.
Emeritus Professor of Mission
Trinity Evangelical Divinity School
Deerfield, Illinois

For more information about
David Sitton
&
Reckless Abandon
please visit:

www.toeverytribe.com
office@toeverytribe.com
@davidsitton

....

For more information about
AMBASSADOR INTERNATIONAL
please visit:

www.ambassador-international.com
@AmbassadorIntl
www.facebook.com/AmbassadorIntl